Living Worship

Cover: Kionsom Waterfall, Sabah
Photograph: Henry K Y Chin

Living Worship

A Learner's Guide to Leading Worship
New Revised Edition

David R. Burfield

Pustaka SUFES Sdn Bhd

Copyright © David R. Burfield 1992 and 2003
All rights reserved

First Edition published 1992
by *DaRBy Publications*, Nottingham
Reprinted 1994

New revised Edition published 2003
by *Pustaka SUFES Sdn Bhd, Kuala Lumpur*

Malaysia National Library Cataloguing-in-Publication Data
Living Worship
ISBN 983-2762-00-6

All Scripture quotations in this publication are from the HOLY BIBLE, NEW INTERNATIONAL VERSION © NIV Copyright 1973, 1978, 1984 by the International Bible Society.

Trade Distributors

Malaysia and Singapore

Pustaka SUFES Sdn Bhd
386 Jalan 5/59, 46000 Petaling Jaya,
Selangor, MALAYSIA
Tel: 03-77828239 Fax: 03-77816599 E-mail: pusufes@po.jaring.my

United Kingdom

Moorley's Print and Publishing
23 Park Road, Ilkeston, Derbys. DE7 5DA, UK
Tel/ Fax: 0115 932 0643   E-mail: info@moorleys.co.uk

Printed in Malaysia by
Academe Art & Printing Services Sdn Bhd, Kuala Lumpur

Dedication

To Ian and Dick, who first threw me in the deep-end of worship leading and preaching, whilst an undergraduate at Manchester. To Michael Baughen, then rector of *Holy Trinity (Platt)*, Rusholme and subsequently Bishop of Chester, who first opened my eyes to the richness of liturgical worship. To my brothers and sisters in Christ at *Sungai-Way Subang Methodist Church* in Kuala Lumpur, with whom I explored the potential of informal worship within the intimacy of a house church fellowship. To the staff, local preachers and worship leaders of the *Long Eaton Methodist Circuit*, together with whom I worshipped and served in nine churches. To the pastors and members of the *Sidang Injil Borneo (SIB)* with whom I have experienced something of the depths of Charismatic worship. To my colleagues and students at *Sabah Theological Seminary* as we work together to build God's kingdom. To Rhona, my wife, who has been my constant inspiration and helper over the precious years we have worshipped together.

Acknowledgement

The author owes a debt of gratitude to a good friend, Roy Tomkinson, who painstakingly proof-read the entire manuscript and provided encouragement and helpful suggestions.

Contents

Preface *(New Edition)*		viii
Preface *(First Edition)*		x
1 – Preliminaries	Worship and living	1
2 – Principles	Holistic worship	15
3 – Patterns	Structure and content	33
4 – Prayer	Leading prayer in worship	55
5 – Preaching	Worship and preaching	73
6 – Praise	Approaches to praise	87
7 – Participation	The people's worship	107
8 – Place	The worship centre	133
9 – Preparation	Preparing the order of worship	155
10 – Presentation	What to say and how to say it	167
11 – Personal	Personal matters for the leader	187
12 – Perspectives	Contemporary worship styles	197
Postscript		211
Bibliography		212

Preface

New Revised Edition

Some ten years have passed since the first edition of *Living Worship* was published and this new edition is long overdue. Whereas the original publication was rapidly put together in a matter of weeks, this new edition has taken much longer to complete and is much more thorough in its treatment. Three chapters have been added. These deal with the vital relationship of worship to daily living, the connection between worship and preaching, and the expression of praise. At the same time, all of the original chapters have been rewritten, updated and expanded with much additional material, including footnotes and brief bibliography.

The original preface has been included both as a reminder of the historical context in which the first edition was written and because the motivation and aims in writing this book remain essentially the same. Thus the main aim of *Living Worship* is to provide a practical guide to all those involved in leading worship.

Worship continues to be at the forefront of the Church's life. The Nineties saw a steady flow of liturgical revisions in mainline churches and a growing number of worship events and training seminars amongst Charismatic churches. There is increasing recognition of the role of the worship leader as distinct from the preacher and this has led to training courses specifically focussed on worship leading. For example, the Methodist Church in Britain has recognised the distinctive role of worship leaders alongside the local preacher

Over the past ten years the influence of the Charismatic renewal on worship has continued to grow, but there is some evidence that the original life and vitality is beginning to ebb. Whereas the outward style of worship remains the same, and worship leaders and musicians have become increasingly professional, there seems to be less awareness of the Spirit at work in worship, together with a hidden longing for a fresh wave of the Spirit to carry worship to new heights. I believe that, in part, the answer to this concern lies in putting into practice a deeper and more biblical understanding of worship such as is described in the early chapters of this book.

As in the first edition, this is intended as a practical resource for all those involved in leading worship, either as beginners or as mature leaders. The book is progressive in structure beginning with a reflection on the relationship of worship and daily living and a basic understanding of what we are about as we worship. With this foundation in place, we look in turn at patterns of church worship and some of the important ingredients. This is followed by a discussion of how we, as leaders, enable the people to worship, and how this is influenced by the place in which we worship. Subsequently we examine the practical issues of how to prepare and present the worship. The book closes with a reflection on important issues that we need to tackle in our personal lives and an evaluation of contemporary worship styles.

Whereas you may well not agree with all that is written, it is my hope that this book will challenge you to think more deeply about worship and in so doing, to lead it more effectively. May you find wheat amongst the chaff, and pearls within the sea of words. May these inspire and equip you to lead other worshippers into the presence of our Lord and King.

Kota Kinabalu, Sabah   *David R. Burfield*
Chinese New Year, 2003

Preface
First Edition

The last few years have seen a revolution in the political systems in Eastern Europe. Whilst few will regret the demise of Communism, many must be concerned at the anarchy that threatens to engulf the former Eastern Block countries. A somewhat similar revolution has taken place in the arena of Christian worship. All over the world the charismatic renewal has swept the Christian church, apparently liberating worship from the tyranny of liturgy and priests and opening congregations to the freedom of the Spirit. But is all well? Are we wise to completely cast aside the order and discipline of liturgical worship and embrace the seeming chaos and often individualism of liberated worship?

These questions are of vital importance since worship is at the heart of all Christian experience. Thus it is arguable that worship is: the central activity of the church; the focal centre of fellowship; the powerhouse for service; the channel for healing and renewal; the means through which we approach God and know God; our ultimate destiny as believers! This book is written in recognition of the centrality of worship in the life of the church and the realisation that the worship leader carries a major responsibility with regard to the direction and efficacy of that worship. At heart, this book seeks not to debate the relative merits of liturgical/ free worship, but rather to explore how our worship, whatever our traditions, theology, or experience, can be truly *living worship*.

Over the years many excellent books have been written concerning the theology of worship or providing historical accounts of the development of liturgy. Other books focus on the musical or choral aspects of worship, but very little has been published which focuses exclusively on the worship leader. It is this gap that the present work seeks to fill. Consequently, little space in this volume is devoted to discuss the theological, historical or musical aspects of worship. Instead, the contents are centred on the worship leader and his/her preparation and presentation. The intention is to provide a thoroughly practical publication, an aid to those leading or preparing to lead worship.

This leads naturally to the sub-title of this monograph: "A Learner's Guide to Leading Worship". Note, this is not specifically a *beginner's* guide, although hopefully a beginner will find much that is helpful. It is a *learner's* guide! As such it is designed for those who realise that the Christian pilgrimage is a learner's road, with no graduation this side of heaven. Consequently, it is my hope that even experienced worship leaders may stumble across some gem, or be reminded of some important principle that has perhaps become blurred by the onset of professionalism. It is a learner's guide in a second sense too. I am with you on that learner's road and write not from the elevated heights of expertise but as a fellow traveller being constantly surprised by what the Lord has to teach me, often from the most unlikely sources!

Before getting to grips with practicalities, it is probably helpful to spend a moment to reflect what worship actually is, since this will help to crystallise our understanding of the nature of the task of the worship leader. At its most basic, leading worship involves bringing people to encounter and respond to the living God – to know Him and be known by Him. It is preparing a people so that their eyes can be opened to the glory of God. It is enabling, encouraging, directing and participating with them, in such a way, that each one can make a life-embracing response to Him. This is an awesome responsibility that over the years we can begin to take for granted.

From this perspective, leading worship embraces not just formal church services but also the many other occasions on which Christians meet together. The prayer meeting, the fellowship group, the ladies' meeting, the Sunday School class, the evangelistic rally, the celebration evening – all are governed by the same worship principles. Consequently, much of what is discussed here will be of value to all who lead worship whatever the context.

Some people are just plain awkward! That was certainly my feeling when a Methodist minister responded to a survey I was conducting to the effect that he spent 168 hours a week in sermon preparation. The answer was not particularly helpful from the viewpoint of compiling significant statistics, but I now know what he meant! Whereas it has taken just a few weeks to set down the text of this book, nevertheless the contents have evolved and been shaped over nearly 25 years of worship leading in a wide variety of churches and fellowship meetings across two continents. Much of the material has been presented, pulled apart and reassembled through worship seminars and training courses, and I owe a debt of gratitude to all those who have shared their ideas and constructive criticisms. Hopefully, this will be a continuing process in which this book is simply another milestone along the way. Thus the book is not offered as a definitive manual for worship leading, but rather in the hope it may act as a catalyst in encouraging, inspiring and enabling *living worship* to the glory of God.

Kota Kinabalu, Sabah **David R. Burfield**
October 1992

1 – Preliminaries

When, recently, our Bible college built a seven-storey hostel block for our students, nothing seemed to happen for the first six months. Certainly there was a lot of noise and the site became very muddy, but there was no evidence of any structure appearing. The reason for the apparent delay was not incompetence but the drilling of foundations to ensure the structural integrity of the building. The opening chapters of this book have similar intention – to provide a firm foundation on which to build a practical guide to leading worship. However, because the main emphasis of this book is as a practical guide rather than an academic text, the introduction will concentrate on several key issues that are fundamental to leading worship.

This book will not of course be read in a vacuum; you may have read other books on worship; you will certainly be experienced as a worshipper and may already be involved in leading worship. For this reason, it is necessary to begin by exploring how different people use the term 'worship' and to explain how we are going to use it in this guide.

What is worship?

One of the confusing things about the Christian community in the modern world is that worship means different things to different people. In this chapter we are going to briefly examine some of these variant ideas and then see how these views compare with the dominant biblical understanding.

Worship as Praise and Adoration

One of the influences of the Charismatic movement has been the renewed emphasis on praise. Praise is understood to be the very heart of worship – the means by which we experience the presence of God and an instrument by which we gain victory over the enemy. The importance given to praise is seen in the use of the now almost ubiquitous phrase 'praise and worship'. However, this phrase is potentially misleading in that it divorces 'praise' from 'worship', *i.e.*, praise is no longer seen as an integral part of the whole act of worship. Thus worship is understood in the narrow sense of adoration and is normally expressed in quieter, slower tempo songs focussing on our love for God.

In this book the term worship is never restricted to adoration but has a much wider meaning that will become evident shortly. Praise is vitally important in worship but, standing alone, is a pale shadow of the whole.

Worship as Music

Closely related to the renewed emphasis on worship as praise is the idea that worship is mediated through music. Music, it is felt, opens the floodgates for the rivers of the Spirit to flow, it carries us into God's presence, and enables us to articulate our praises. In practice, this concept usually involves an uninterrupted period of continuous music and song, often led by a leader, singers and a music team. Whereas this may be only part of the whole worship service, yet for many it is considered to be 'the worship'.

This apparent dichotomy is evident in an excellent practical book on worship authored by John Leach and entitled: 'Living Liturgy'. The book is written from an Anglican perspective with the intention of showing that the liturgy has a vital role in 'Spirit-led' worship. Nevertheless, in a chapter discussing the musical aspects of leading worship, the writer feels constrained by popular usage to assign two distinct meanings to the term worship:

> "We hope of course, that the whole service will be 'worship', but for many people music is at the heart of their response to God. I don't want to get into any arguments about terminology, so you will need to put up with me using the word 'worship' in two distinct ways: to describe the service or meeting as a whole, but also that part of it commonly designated a 'time of worship' or a 'worship slot'."[1]

---

[1] Leach (1997) p 169

Despite the emphasis on the importance of liturgy throughout the rest of the book, it is difficult to resist the conclusion that Leach has given in to the popular understanding that the heart of worship is song – mediated in a particular way. There is actually no need to surrender the term 'worship' to describe this part of the service since a time of 'praise and adoration' would usually be accurate.

The danger in allowing the term worship to be used in such a way is that it subtly reinforces what some already 'know', that the essence of worship is *singing* God's praises. Thus some liturgical churches precede the liturgy with a 'time of worship', i.e., singing God's praises, and then switch to the 'worship proper', i.e., the liturgy[2]. Such a strategy is a compromise allowing both 'the renewed' and traditionalists to feel they have worshipped.

But there is no actual need to take songs of praise out of the context of liturgy – in fact this is to deny much of the meaning and flow of the liturgical worship. Music and song have a crucial role in bringing life to the liturgy – as an integral part, not as an add-on extra! There is also no need to denude the 'worship slot' of elements such as confession, offering, intercession and hearing God's word.

These comments are not intended in any way to belittle the importance of praise and adoration, nor of the vital role of music in worship[3], but rather to emphasise that they are a *part* and not the *whole* of worship

Worship as Lifestyle

In contemporary books concerned with the renewal of worship there is often an introductory section with titles such as 'Being a Worshipper' or 'A Lifestyle of Worship'[4]. The thrust of these sections is usually that worship should not be confined to the worship service but should spill

---

[2] It is not unusual to actually hear the liturgist say, at the end of a time of praise, words to the effect, "Let us now begin the 'worship proper'," with the meaning "let us now start using the liturgy."

[3] Music is undeniably a powerful medium. For example, the author knows of an elderly lady, unable to speak because of a stroke, but able to join in singing a hymn when accompanied by piano playing.

[4] See, for example, Boschman (1994) p 3

over into our daily living. Such authors point to a variety of scriptural texts that encourage the idea that the Christian life should be a life of praise. Typical of such texts is the following verse from Hebrews[5]:

> "Through Jesus, therefore, let us continually offer to God a sacrifice of praise – the fruit of lips that confess his name." (Hebrews 13:15)

The perceived application is that our life should be one of unceasing praise, wherever we are and whatever our circumstances. Thus Boschman writes:

> "I believe many Christians are seeing the need, as well as having the desire, to develop a lifestyle of worship. The introduction of worship tapes is in direct response to the desire of believers to worship more than in a church building once a week for an hour or two. With these tapes they are able to sing along and let their spirits commune with the Lord any time and any place."[6]

This is actually a very important point. Worship cannot be contained within the four walls of a church building, or the length of a service, or one day a week. However, whereas a life characterised by praise and thanksgiving would be revolutionary for many Christians, there is actually something more fundamental still – *living worship*.

Living Worship

Having glanced briefly at three contemporary understandings of worship, now is the time to explain how the term worship is used in this book and more specifically what is meant by *living worship*.

We are going to use the term 'worship' in two quite distinct yet inter-related ways. The first is that our whole life, the way we live, our lifestyle is to be one continuous act of worship. This embraces both a personal commitment to God as well as a corporate commitment as part of the body of Christ – the Church. We shall develop this idea shortly.

The second meaning of worship is the more restricted sense that refers to the activities contained within a worship service when we meet together as God's people to declare his glory. These activities, whilst

---

[5] Other similar texts include:Psalms 34:1; 35:28; 145:1,2; Eph 5:20

[6] Boschman (1994) p 5

including praise and adoration, also include many other aspects that help us to both build and articulate our relationship with God and one another.

Whereas this book is principally concerned with enabling Christians to lead corporate worship, that is, engaging with the second meaning of worship, yet this cannot be done without understanding worship as a way of life. Our acts of corporate worship spring from our daily lives, and feed back into our daily lives. How we worship on a Sunday is largely dependent on how we have lived during the week. How we live during the week, in turn, should be influenced and transformed by our act of worship.

The phrase *living worship* has thus a double meaning. Firstly, it is active, describing the heart of what it means to be a Christian. We live as an act of worship. Secondly, it is descriptive, referring to the quality of worship that we aim to celebrate together. Our desire is that worship should not be just a routine, a habit, an empty tradition, but a living entity. We long that our worship should come alive, that our lives should be touched and changed, that we might fellowship with the living God. Essentially that worship would be a reality rather than pretence or show.

The main emphasis in this book is the pivotal role of the worship leader in helping worshippers come alive to God – to experience *living worship*. This can only be done as we understand the foundations of worship. To this we now turn.

Life – An act of worship

At its most fundamental, *living worship* is just that – living as an act of worship. This is more than living with praise on our lips and a song in our heart – it is living for God. The things we do and say, our work, our families, our ambitions, our motivation and our aspirations are for God. Paul put it succinctly when he wrote to the Philippian Christians from his prison cell:

"For me, to live is Christ and to die is gain."   (Phil 1:19)

Many years before, on Paul's first evangelistic visit to Philippi, he and his co-worker Silas were arrested, stripped, severely beaten and thrown into prison. Their response? An impromptu praise and prayer meeting at midnight.[7] Why? Because their lives were totally committed to God and they believed God had plan and purpose behind what had happened. They lived as an act of worship.

When I became a Christian at the age of thirteen I was consistently near the bottom of my form at school. I was in the dunces' class. Within two years I was topping the exam results. Why? Not because God unjustly provided me the answers to the exams but because I learned to study to his praise and glory. My studies became an act of worship, an expression of love to my Lord who had rescued me from darkness.

A Biblical Basis for Living Worship

The above idea is so important as it has such a profound effect on the way we worship and lead others to worship. For this reason I intend to outline in some detail the biblical basis of *living worship*.

Biblical Terminology

The idea that worship is more than just a Sunday activity derives from the various words in the original biblical languages that are translated into English as worship[8]. Amongst the half a dozen or so words are those that emphasise: God's glory and awesomeness; our response as we bow down before our Mighty King in homage, fear and respect; and our response in serving him as Lord.

A reference to the third aspect is found in our use of the term 'worship service'. This is a reminder that worship involves serving God. For example, Jesus rejects the devil's temptation to bow down and worship him with the words:

"Worship the Lord your God, and serve him only." (Mat 4:10)

Two distinct Greek words for worship are used in this passage, the first one emphasising the reverence due to God as the ruler of this world, the second one emphasising worship as the act of service of a slave or a

---

[7] See Acts 16:16-40 for the full account.

[8] The original text of the Old Testament is largely Hebrew with some Aramaic. The New Testament was written in Greek.

Preliminaries 7

paid servant. Paul uses the same word as he challenges his readers in Rome to:

> "...offer your bodies as living sacrifices, holy and pleasing to God—this is your spiritual act of worship."   (Rom 12:1)

This is essentially a call for commitment to life-long service.

A further reminder of servanthood is our use of the word liturgy. This actually derives from a Greek word that literally means 'the people's work' but is usually translated as worship. This word is used to describe the gathering together of the Antioch Christians in prayer and fasting[9] as well as the practical ministry of Gentile Christians in providing financial support for their impoverished Jewish brethren[10].

To worship God is thus not only to sing his praises but to live in his service – living worship.

The Prophetic Critique of Worship

The Old Testament prophets make it plain that the essence of worship lies not in the externals of sacrifice and celebration of festivals – although these were important – but in lives lived out faithfully in God's service.

Beyond sacrifice

When Saul and the Israelite army defeated the Amalekites they were commanded to kill all the livestock. However, the animals were kept alive with the excuse that they would be offered as a sacrifice to God. The prophet Samuel rejected this flimsy excuse, declaring:

> "Does the Lord delight in burnt offerings and sacrifices as much as in obeying the voice of the Lord? To obey is better than sacrifice, and to heed is better than the fat of rams."   (1 Samuel 15:22)

Saul needed to learn that obedience was more important than religious ritual.

Saul's successor King David also had to learn this truth. Following his adultery with Bathsheba and the murder of Uriah, David is confronted

---

[9] Acts 13:2
[10] Romans 15:27

by the prophet Nathan and brought to realise the depth of his unfaithfulness to God. The new depth of understanding shines through the psalm that reflects on this incident in which he writes of God:

> "You do not delight in sacrifice, or I would bring it; you do not take pleasure in burnt offerings. The sacrifices of God are a broken spirit; a broken and a contrite heart, O God, you will not despise." (Ps 51:16,17)

The prophet Micah came to a very similar conclusion that there was something more important than thousands of sacrifices or rivers of oil offered to God:

> "He has showed you, O man, what is good. And what does the LORD require of you? To act justly and to love mercy and to walk humbly with your God. (Micah 6:8)

Each of these passages show quite clearly that true, acceptable worship is inseparable from our attitudes, our actions and our lives. We please God not through extravagant and excessive ritual but in lives lived in humble obedience to his will.

Beyond celebration

But of course it is not just the Israelite kings that came under fire from the prophets, it was the people themselves. Isaiah's critique of worship begins in the very first chapter of this long prophetic book. In quick succession the Lord rejects: sacrifices and burnt offerings (v 11); offerings of incense (v 13); Sabbaths, festivals and celebrations (v 13,14); and even their many prayers (v 15).

However, it is not the religious acts of worship that are at fault, it is the people's unholy, corrupt and uncaring lifestyle which renders their worship meaningless and unacceptable to God. Thus the Lord describes their lifestyle:

> "... Your hands are full of blood; wash and make yourselves clean. Take your evil deeds out of my sight! Stop doing wrong, learn to do right! Seek justice, encourage the oppressed. Defend the cause of the fatherless, plead the case of the widow." (Isaiah 1:15-17)

The people's worship is rejected because they live their daily lives as strangers to God. A very similar criticism is found in chapter 58 of the same prophecy where the Lord explains that he ignores their prayer and

Preliminaries

fasting because of the breakdown of community life and lack of care and compassion for the weak and helpless. They are continuously quarrelling and fighting one another and indifferent to the needs within society.[11]

The people's fasting consists in outward observance but with a heart far from God. The fasting (worship) that is acceptable to God is quite distinct:

> "Is not this the kind of fasting I have chosen: to loose the chains of injustice and untie the cords of the yoke, to set the oppressed free and break every yoke? Is it not to share your food with the hungry and to provide the poor wanderer with shelter— when you see the naked, to clothe him, and not to turn away from your own flesh and blood?"
>
> (Isaiah 58:6,7)

Very similar criticisms are found in the prophecy of Amos where the people had become rich through exploitation of the weak and marginalized in society – the poor, the sick, the widowed, the orphaned, and the foreigner. In a very dramatic passage the Lord completely rejects their worship with the words:

> "I hate, I despise your religious feasts; I cannot stand your assemblies. Even though you bring me burnt offerings and grain offerings, I will not accept them. Though you bring choice fellowship offerings, I will have no regard for them. Away with the noise of your songs! I will not listen to the music of your harps. But let justice roll on like a river, righteousness like a never-failing stream!" (Amos 5:21-24)

The above passage is a remarkable rejection of every aspect of the people's worship: their feasts and special celebrations; their offerings and sacrifices; their singing and their music. It is one that we cannot afford to ignore if we want to offer worship that is acceptable to God.

Clearly, what makes our acts of worship acceptable to God is not the professional way in which they are led or offered, nor our skills and eloquence, but the beauty and holiness of our lives. In this particular case, Amos pleads not for generosity or kindness but for justice.

---

[11] See especially: Is 58:3-7

The Teaching of Jesus

Jesus too stands in the stream of Old Testament prophecy and on several occasions his teaching, stories and actions challenge the worship life of the Jewish community of his time.

On very many occasions Jesus emphasises that it is not the ritual or outward action that is important but the intention of the heart. Thus Jesus gives the example of someone offering his or her gift at the altar who has hurt someone else[12]. For Jesus, the offering is meaningless whilst hatred still burns in the worshipper's heart. A similar thought is contained in the wise answer of one of the teachers of the law in conversation with Jesus:

> "To love him (God) with all your heart, with all your understanding and with all your strength, and to love your neighbor as yourself is more important than all burnt offerings and sacrifices." (Mark 12:33)

Inevitably our acts of worship cannot be divorced from our daily living.

In other passages[13] Jesus confronts the teachers of the law and the Pharisees because, whereas they were scrupulous in observing their worship obligation of tithing, yet they neglected the more important issues of justice, mercy and faithfulness. Sometimes they became so zealous for their religious obligation of giving that they neglected to care and provide for their parents[14]. Such behaviour causes Jesus to apply to them the words of the prophet Isaiah[15]:

> "These people honor me with their lips, but their hearts are far from me. They worship me in vain; their teachings are but rules taught by men."
> (Mat 15:8,9)

Here again, the key to worship is not just prescribed actions or pleasing words but a heart that truly seeks to honour God.

Jesus' stories and observations also provide an insight into his understanding of true worship. For example, Jesus tells the story of two

---

[12] Matthew 5:23,24
[13] Mat 23:23; Luke 11:42
[14] Mat 15:3-9
[15] Isaiah 29:13

Preliminaries

men who went to the temple to pray[16]. The first, a Pharisee, tells God about his personal goodness, his acts of worship – his giving and his fasting. The second is distraught before God, he has nothing to commend him; he simply cries from the heart: "God, have mercy on me a sinner." In Jesus' view it is this second man that has really worshipped.

Jesus' teaching and stories are of course accompanied by action. One of the most controversial was when Jesus threw out the street traders and moneychangers from the temple[17] with the words:

> "It is written," he said to them, "My house will be called 'a house of prayer,' but you are making it a 'den of robbers.'" (Mat 21:13)

At first sight Jesus' action is quite extraordinary as the people thrown out were providing a service to pilgrims to enable them to offer sacrifices. But in reality the merchants and traders were cheating the visitors and changing the outer courts of the temple – reserved for Gentile god-fearers – into little better than a common market place. Deceit, cheating and corruption threatened to undermine the whole of the temple worship.

Other New Testament Teaching

There are several key texts in the New Testament that are always quoted in discussions of worship. Whereas the texts themselves are important, their context[18] often provides a greater depth of meaning.

The first key verse from Hebrews is often used to emphasise that worship as a way of life means a life of unceasing praise. The verse states:

> "Through Jesus, therefore, let us continually offer to God a sacrifice of praise—the fruit of lips that confess his name." (Hebrews 13:15)

The Hebrews' writer's use of the language of sacrifice makes clear that praise is connected with our worship of God and that praise should come naturally to the lips of those who claim Jesus as Lord of their

---

[16] Luke 18:9-14

[17] Mat 21:12,13; Mark 11:15-17; Luke 19:45-46

[18] Context refers to the whole passage surrounding the particular verse in question.

lives. True, Christians should be a 'people of praise' but this is not the whole story! The very next verse continues:

> "And do not forget to do good and to share with others, for with such sacrifices God is pleased." (Hebrews 13:16)

Thus it is not only the 'sacrifice of praise' that is required from Christians but the sacrifices of 'doing good' and 'sharing with others'. If one looked a little further in the same chapter, the list of 'sacrifices' is expanded to include: hospitality, caring for prisoners, faithfulness in marriage, contentment, and submission to authority. In other words, our worship is not solely about praise; it is the very way we live our lives.

Paul's challenge to the Christians in Rome provides another key text in understanding worship as a 'way of life':

> "Therefore, I urge you, brothers, in view of God's mercy, to offer your bodies as living sacrifices, holy and pleasing to God—this is your spiritual act of worship." (Romans 12:1)

Again an examination of the context of the verse helps us to see that what Paul is talking about is an act of worship that embraces the whole of our life. To begin with, this commitment means we should not conform to the standards and behaviour of the secular world around us (v 2). Such commitment also means that we should live actively as part of the 'body of Christ' (vs 4-8) and learn to live in a Christ-like way in the wider society amongst friends and enemies alike (vs 9-21).

Yet another key verse comes in Peter's first letter written to believers scattered throughout Asia Minor. Here he reminds them of their status and primary task:

> "But you are a chosen people, a royal priesthood, a holy nation, a people belonging to God, that you may declare the praises of him who called you out of darkness into his wonderful light." (1 Peter 2:9)

As God's royal priesthood, their act of worship is to 'declare his praises'. But what does this actually mean? Certainly it needs to be taken literally, that is we need to praise God with our lips whether in a worship service or outside the church. But it is not just our lips but also our lives that need to declare his praises. This is evident in the verses that follow:

> "Live such good lives among the pagans that, though they accuse you of doing wrong, they may see your good deeds and glorify God on the day he visits us." (1 Peter 2:12)

The final example is taken from the letter of James. James is concerned with the practical problem of taming the tongue. He pinpoints a particularly inconsistency that trips up many Christians:

> "With the tongue we praise our Lord and Father, and with it we curse men, who have been made in God's likeness. Out of the same mouth come praise and cursing. My brothers, this should not be." (James 3:9,10)

Clearly, our worship of God needs to be in tune with our relationship with others. It is inconsistent to bless God and then almost in the same breath bad mouth our fellow Christians, our family, our work-mates or even our enemies.

Conclusions

In this chapter, although I have not pinpointed a specific definition of worship, yet it should be clear that worship for the Christian involves far more than meeting with other believers on a Sunday. Worship is about lives lived in pleasing God. Thus *living worship* carries a double meaning:

> ➤ It is firstly the desire of our hearts as God's children that our very lives should be lived as an act of worship so as to bring glory to God.
> ➤ It is secondly a statement of intent for our worship service – that the worship is alive.

But, of course, as noted earlier, these are not really separable. The Scriptures clearly show that for worship to be alive, to be acceptable to God, to be touched and empowered by God, then our lives must be lived for him. Our Sunday worship must be an integral part of our lives and not an optional add-on extra. To put things another way, the quality of the worshippers will affect the quality of the worship[19].

---

[19] This is an aspect well understood by preachers. Some congregations empower the preaching by their presence – there is an eagerness to hear God's word and an openness to receive. Other congregations quench the preaching by their absence – wandering thoughts, conversations, looks of boredom.

From the viewpoint of leading a worship service, it is very important to understand the inter-relationship between the service and the lives of the worshippers. There is a two-way relationship: the worshippers will bring their lives to the worship and this will affect the worship; the worship in turn will touch the worshippers and this will affect their lives.

Therefore, the worship service needs to be designed and led in such a way that the worshippers can bring their lives to worship, and the worship will speak to their lives. Through *living worship* lives are touched, challenged, changed, healed, renewed, encouraged and equipped for future service in the world. The Sunday worship can either be considered as the climax of a week's worship activity or the beginning of a new week of *living worship*. Thus the Methodist Holy Communion service[20] ends with this prayer:

> *Go in peace in the power of the Spirit*
> *to live and work to God's praise and glory.*
> **Thanks be to God. Amen.**

---

[20] *The Methodist Worship Book* (1999) p 197

2 - Principles

On one occasion Jesus was asked to name the most important commandment and He replied:

> "Love the Lord your God with all your heart and with all your soul and with all your mind and with all your strength." [Mark 12:30]

This verse is a key to understanding worship since there is a very close connection between love and worship. For example, it is sometimes said of someone very much in love: "He worships the ground she stands on." To love God is to worship Him and even to reverence the place where God is encountered.[1] Likewise, true worship must necessarily spring from a motivation of love.[2]

With this close connection in mind, it is probably not too much a distortion of the spirit of the text quoted above to consider that as believers we are called to: worship God with all our heart, soul, mind and strength. In other words we are called to holistic worship encompassing our whole being: our feelings, our understanding, our character, our personality, our will, our spiritual nature, our physical bodies, our talents and gifts. All that we are, our whole person, is called into relationship with God within worship.

Whereas it is sometimes helpful to describe our human nature in terms of heart, soul, mind and body in order to emphasise certain aspects, we need to hold on to an holistic understanding of what it means to be human. By this we mean that our humanity cannot be separated into distinct and unrelated self-existing components. For example, the Bible

---

[1] For example, after Jacob's heavenly vision he names the place Bethel – meaning house of God - and erects a memorial stone (Gen 28:10-22). Similarly, when Moses meets with God at the burning bush he removes his shoes out of respect because he is standing on 'holy ground'. (Ex 3:5).

[2] Elsewhere in his letter to the church in Corinth Paul makes it plain that the motivation of love is the essential component of meaningful service – see 1 Cor 13:1-3.

knows nothing of a disembodied soul.[3] Furthermore, it is evident that our physical bodies, our minds and our feelings are interactive. For example, if we are overtired, then this affects our feelings and we may become irritable and moody. Similarly, if we are grieving the loss of a loved one, it may be very difficult to think straight and cope with simple administrative tasks.[4] Tiredness or exhaustion may also affect our relationship with God.[5]

Thus the essence of Jesus' words, a quotation incidentally from Deut 6:5, is that we are to love God, and by analogy, to worship Him, with the whole of our being and resources. A somewhat similar idea is evident in Paul's letter to the believers in Rome, where he urges them:

> "... offer your bodies as living sacrifices, holy and pleasing to God - this is your spiritual act of worship." [Romans 12:1]

Paul is urging the Roman Christians to consecrate their lives totally to God, to be used in his service.

Therefore, the first thing we need to grasp as worship leaders is that living worship is holistic, involving the whole of our being and our lives in relationship to God. Let's see what this means in practice.

The Whole Person

Regrettably many worship services do not permit, let alone enable or encourage, the participation of the whole person. On the one hand, liturgical worship tends to feed our minds but starve our emotions. On the other hand, charismatic worship enables free expression of our feelings but often at the expense of understanding. Neither extreme is

---

[3] Thus in Paul's discussion of the resurrection (1 Cor 15) it is clear that this does not involve the soul parting from the body but rather being equipped with a new spiritual body (v 44).

[4] Grief is perhaps one of the reasons that Mary Magdalene did not recognise the risen Christ (John 20:10-18).

[5] See, for example, the experience of Elijah (1 Kings 18,19). Elijah had just reached the climax of his career with a triumphant victory over the prophets of Baal on Mount Carmel. After his victory Elijah is forced to flee for his life and, in a state of physical exhaustion and fear, he loses confidence in God and hopes only for death (1 Kings 19:4).

Principles

holistic worship. Such worship requires the involvement of the whole person, and must include the aspects alluded to in Jesus' summary of the way in which we should love God. To these we now turn.

All our heart

Firstly, we are called to worship God with all our heart.[6] In a Western context the heart is the symbol of feeling and emotion and it is with this meaning it is used here.[7] Love that never revealed or expressed itself with feeling or emotion is almost unimaginable. Similarly, worship without feeling is a caricature of biblical worship. Admittedly the way in which we express our feelings publicly depends on our cultural background and upbringing[8], but, nevertheless, the complete suppression of any display of emotion is unbiblical.

Expressing feelings in the Bible

For example, the book of Psalms[9] – the Jewish equivalent of a song or worship book – is overflowing with references to the outpouring of emotion within private devotion or public worship. The psalmist openly expresses feelings such as: anger, despair, sorrow, awe, wonder, humility, joy, praise and thankfulness. Thus it is difficult to read Psalm 51 without being made aware of the depth of sorrow that David feels as a consequence of his sin. Or, Psalm 42, where the psalmist compares his heartfelt longing for God to the desperate search of the thirsty deer

---

[6] In the Hebrew understanding the heart has more to do with the will and understanding. However, as the intent of Jesus' quotation is to refer to our complete human nature, it is not inappropriate to discuss using Western categories.

[7] It is interesting to note how in different cultures different parts of the body are considered the seat of the emotions. In Hebrew understanding it is the 'bowels' that represent emotion, whereas in Malay or Indonesian it is the 'liver'.

[8] Examples are seen in the British obsession with the 'stiff upper lip', taught and reinforced by gender-specific comments such as 'big boys don't cry'. The Chinese reputation of being inscrutable is also related to cultural suppression of visible emotion.

[9] The book of Psalms is an amazing compilation of songs of worship with a wide variety of themes. Many different authors were involved probably over a period of around 1000 years. The psalms were central to the worship life of the Jewish people, including Jesus and his disciples. The use of the term 'the psalmist' is not meant to imply that one person wrote the psalms but is a useful shorthand when the specific writer is uncertain.

for water in the arid desert.[10] The psalmist, probably writing in exile far from the holy city Jerusalem, is moved to tears (v 3) as he remembers the joyful vibrant worship of former years (v 4).

Similarly, in very many psalms, the psalmist encourages the people to praise God with an outward display of feeling: with clapping hands and cries of joy [Psalm 47:1]; with shouting and singing [Psalm 66:1,2]; with shouts of joy and stirring music [Psalm 98:4-6]; with music and dancing [Psalm 150]. Of course, emotional expression in worship is not limited to the psalms. Miriam and 'all the women' celebrated the defeat of Pharaoh's army with songs and tambourine dancing.[11] Again King David celebrated the arrival of the 'ark of the covenant' to Jerusalem accompanied by the people's shouts, choral singing, the sounding of trumpets and other loud musical instruments together with dancing.[12]

Although not too much is said in the gospels about Jesus' public expression of feeling, there are several important clues. First, he almost certainly had a keen sense of humour. Many of his pithy sayings take the form of puns or absurdities.[13] One can hardly resist the conclusion that sometimes Jesus had his hearers 'rolling in the aisles'. However, at times Jesus also showed a stern face. He publicly rebuked his over-zealous disciples who were busy turning away the women and children; and expressed his anger at the cheats and traders who were turning the temple into a market place.[14]

Jesus also had a more tender side. On arriving at Bethany after the death of Lazarus he is moved to tears by the grief of Mary and Martha at the loss of their brother. John records that publicly, in full view of the

---

[10] In Palestine during the dry season before the rains the desert streams dry up and the wild animals engage in a desperate search for life-giving water.

[11] See Exodus 15:20-21

[12] See 1 Chron 15:25-29

[13] For example, the critical brother inspecting the speck of sawdust in his brother's eye aided by a log protruding from his own (Mat 7:3-5). Or, the religious leaders busy straining out a gnat while all the time swallowing a camel (Mat 23:24). Or the story of the Good Samaritan where the hero is a hated foreigner and the religious people are the villains (Luke 10:25-37).

[14] Matthew 21:12-17

Principles

bystanders, 'Jesus wept'.[15] Another emotional episode for Jesus, this time recorded by Luke, occurred at his triumphal entry into Jerusalem. Although the crowds welcomed him in royal fashion with shouts of acclamation, Jesus knew that before long the people represented by their spiritual leaders would reject him and the good news of the coming kingdom. Jesus wept over the city in the knowledge that their rejection would have catastrophic consequences for themselves and the holy city.[16]

Expressing feelings in worship

Because our emotions are God given and are an integral part of who we are they are an important part of *living worship*. As worship leaders we need to explore the full range of emotions and consider how they can rightly be expressed in the context of worship. Thus worship should involve us in an awareness of awe and wonder, emotions of joy and sorrow, feelings of love, peace and security. In circumstances where people feel unable[17] to freely express emotion, the content of the worship service can help. Aspects such as: music, silence, beauty or stirring speech may often be conducive to bringing release in this area.

However, it is vitally important that emotional expression should be genuine and spontaneous, not contrived or whipped up to suit the occasion. This means that the worship leader is sensitive to the people's condition and feelings and leads them to express them appropriately rather than attempting to impose feelings that are completely alien to their situation.[18] For example, at a funeral service the dominant emotion at the beginning of the service would normally be a feeling of sorrow and loss. This should find expression in the worship: in the introductory comments, scripture text, prayer and the choice of hymn. However, the

---

[15] John 11:35 – In the text the bystanders interpret Jesus' tears to his great love for Lazarus, but as he was about to raise him from the dead it is perhaps more likely that the tears were empathetic with the feelings of loss of the two sisters.

[16] Luke 19:41-44

[17] Sometimes people may need release or healing from the inability to express emotion. Right expression of emotion is cathartic; for example, the ability to cry at the loss of a loved one is part of the natural grieving process that should not be repressed.

[18] The leader must also be sensitive to the prompting of the Holy Spirit.

worshipper can be moved on emotionally through the service from grief at the loss of a loved one, to a sense of peace at God's presence, to a deep down joy and thankfulness that the loved one is with Christ, which is far better.

Just occasionally, especially in the more charismatic traditions, leaders tend to impose feelings on the congregation. For example, the leader may begin the service with a question to the worshippers such as: "Do you have joy in your heart this morning?" (This is often not a genuine question since the assumed answer is yes.) The people are then directed to express that joy by some outward sign.[19] If the expression is half-hearted, the congregation may then be scolded for lack of enthusiasm. This misunderstanding occurs because, whereas it is biblical for Christians to experience the 'joy of the Lord', we may not always be feeling it. At the beginning of a service there may be a multitude of reasons why we are not feeling joyful – unconfessed sin, sorrow, tiredness, worldly distractions and so on. It is for the leader to understand the people's experience and to lead them on into the presence of the Lord where joy abounds.[20]

It should be evident that an emotional dimension of worship is biblical. However, leading the congregation to express their feelings to God must be done sensitively and in such a way that the emotions are genuinely expressed and become an integral part of our worship.

All our soul

Secondly, we are called to worship God with all our soul. This reminds us that worship is far more than just an expression of feeling; it has a spiritual dimension. Whereas scientific studies suggest that humanity is closely connected to other living creatures on this planet, this is not the complete picture.[21] Thus the Bible records a remarkable truth:

---

[19] The congregation might be invited to raise their hands, to give a 'clap offering' or to shout some acclamation of praise. The danger is that if you do not feel joyful and yet respond you are in effect play-acting – giving a response which is not genuine.

[20] Psalm 16:11

[21] The physical similarities between humankind and the rest of the animal kingdom are hardly surprising from the viewpoint of a common environment and the same creator.

Principles

> "So God created man in his own image, in the image of God he created him; male and female he created them." [Genesis 1:27]

It is evident from this verse that people, both men and women, are special and distinct from the animal kingdom as they are created 'in the image of God'. Exactly what this phrase means is not clear but quite possibly it refers to the fact that men and women are spiritual creatures and it is this that separates us from the rest of the animal kingdom.

It is precisely because we are spiritual creatures that we can enter into a close relation with God who is spirit. Thus Jesus in conversation with the Samaritan woman tells her:

> "Yet a time is coming and has now come when the true worshipers will worship the Father in spirit and truth, for they are the kind of worshipers the Father seeks. God is spirit, and his worshipers must worship in spirit and in truth." (John 4:23,24)

There is thus a spiritual element to worship that goes beyond our understanding and feelings and allows us in an intangible way to communicate with God. This is hinted at in the words of the prophet Isaiah:

> "For my thoughts are not your thoughts, neither are your ways my ways... As the heavens are higher than the earth, so are my ways higher than your ways and my thoughts than your thoughts." [Isaiah 55:8,9]

These words are not intended to convey the meaning that it is impossible to relate to God since they are written in the context of the call to: 'Seek the Lord' (v.6). Rather they remind us that we cannot come to God through our intellect alone.

In the New Testament it is the Holy Spirit who mediates our worship and enables us to approach God in the intimacy of the 'Abba, Father' relationship.[22] This emphasis on the spiritual nature of worship reminds us that even in worship we are dependent upon the grace of God. In practical terms this teaches us that preparing for worship is more than just a routine of planning and selection of the ingredients of worship. It involves a spiritual preparation through prayer and perhaps fasting. It is a preparation that begins much earlier than the opening prayer or hymn of praise; a preparation begun on our knees alone and together

---

[22] Romans 8:15

with our fellow worshipers. How vital it is that church prayer meetings and fellowship groups should regularly pray for the Sunday worship!

But it also means, and this is something that we learn from the scriptures[23], that we should be open to the use of spiritual gifts in worship. Those that are especially relevant in the context of worship include: words of knowledge, prophecy, healing, tongues with interpretation.[24] Most of these gifts can be appropriately introduced in fairly traditional parts of the worship service such as: preaching, testimony, or prayer ministry, but in a way which is 'fitting and orderly'.[25] Whereas the Spirit cannot be commanded, we can allow for his gifts to be used or restrict his working. For example, a time of prayer for healing enables the healing gift to be used. A time of testimony provides opportunity for the Spirit to speak through the whole body of Christ and not just the appointed leaders.[26]

It is very important to understand that spiritual worship is not the same as emotional worship. Thus it is not necessary to weep or be laughing or shouting with joy to experience the powerful presence of the Spirit.[27] The Spirit is often present in the calm as the 'still small voice'.[28] However, sometimes our response to the Spirit's presence may well be emotionally tinged. For example, those brought under conviction of sin by the Spirit may well respond in tears of sorrow[29], those healed may hardly be able to contain their joy and thankfulness.[30] But sadly, all too often the reality of the Spirit's power and presence is substituted by

---

[23] See Paul's extensive discussion in 1 Corinthians chs 12-14.

[24] The gift of 'speaking in tongues' is generally understood to be more for personal edification and is thus less appropriate to corporate worship unless the meaning is interpreted.

[25] 1 Cor 14:40

[26] This is not about democracy but the biblical truth that the Spirit indwells, gives gifts to and uses the whole body of Christ – the congregation.

[27] Note it was the false prophets of Baal who felt constrained to shout, to dance and frantically prophesy in order to communicate with their 'god'. Elijah only had to pray in a calm clear voice to see God answer in power. (1 Kings 18:26-29, 36,37.)

[28] 1 Kings 19:12

[29] Nehemiah 8:9

[30] Acts 3:8

induced and artificial emotion. This is not spiritual or Spirit-led worship.

All our mind

Thirdly, we are called to worship God with our entire mind. The mind emphasises that worship is also a rational process. We need to use our minds as we prepare worship and lead in such a way that we encourage our fellow worshipers to think about God. Thus in writing to the Christians at Philippi Paul encouraged them with the words:

> "Finally, brothers, whatever is true, whatever is noble, whatever is right, whatever is pure, whatever is lovely, whatever is admirable - if anything is excellent or praise-worthy – *think* about such things. " [Philippians 4:8]

Our worship should enable people to reflect about God and to fill their minds with things which are true, noble, right, pure, lovely... .

Elsewhere, in the context of worship, Paul challenges the believers:

> "Do not conform any longer to the pattern of this world, but be transformed by the renewing of your mind." [Romans 12:2]

Day by day the Christian is bombarded by secular worldviews that threaten to become the pattern for living.[31] Our Christian worship must challenge and feed the mind, leading to renewal of our way of thinking and transformation of our daily lives. Worship that only stirs the emotions but fails to feed the mind will do little to prepare the people for *living worship*.

The psalmist was also acutely aware of the importance of rational worship. Thus many of the stirring worship psalms, which encourage the congregation to a riot of praise and thanksgiving, are brimming with reasons why we should praise. In so doing the psalms combine an appeal to both the heart and mind. A typical example is Psalm 100. In the opening two verses of this brief psalm the writer calls the people to heartfelt emotive worship:

> "Shout for joy to the LORD, all the earth. Worship the LORD with gladness; come before him with joyful songs."

---

[31] For example, the content of the media, whether drama, documentary, entertainment, news or advertisement are largely dominated by a secular worldview and hence promote values and lifestyles that are sub-Christian in content.

But then in verse 3, the people are reminded of the reasons for their praise:

> "Know the Lord is God. It is He who made us, and we are his; we are His people and the sheep of His pasture."

The cycle is then repeated with another call to praise and thanksgiving (v 4) and further reasons for praise (v 5).

It is apparent that understanding should undergird our feelings. If we know why we are praising God then this invigorates and strengthens our praise and enables our worship to be holistic. It means that our worship is genuine and our feelings an appropriate response to who God is and what he has done for us. An examination of almost any of the traditional hymns of praise reveals that the hymn writer understood the need to base our worship on a knowledge of who God is and what he has done.[32] For example, the Wesleyan Christmas hymn, 'Hark the Herald Angels sing' contains, in a few verses, a doctrinal statement of the nature of Christ – his deity, humanity and the wonder of the incarnation; together with a summary of God's plan of salvation – reconciliation of sinners, new life, healing, and the resurrection. The whole glorious hymn is a vital proclamation of biblical truth set in the context of a hymn of praise.

By contrast, many modern praise songs centre on our feeling and response rather than God's nature, initiative and purpose. For example, a three-verse hymn entitled 'Praise Him' contains the opening lyrics and chorus[33]:

> Praise Him, praise Him, praise Him with your song
> Praise Him, praise Him, and praise Him all day long!
> > *For the Lord is worthy, worthy to receive our praise.*
> > *For the Lord is worthy, worthy to receive our praise.*

---

[32] There was, of course, also the underlying intention to teach correct doctrine and theology through song. Long after the people forget the sermon they will still be seeing (singing?) the songs used in worship.

[33] The song composed by Twila Paris appears as number 463 in *Songs of Fellowship*. Appropriately enough the music is annotated 'With feeling'.

Principles 25

The subsequent two verses are very similar in content, urging the worshipper to praise God with heart and life. The song is thus person-centred, concentrating on our duty to worship and how we should worship. The three verse song teaches us nothing about God apart from the general statement that the 'Lord is worthy'. Such hymns may help us to 'feel' praise – especially if the melody is particularly inspiring – but contributes very little to our understanding of the reasons for our praise.

As worship leaders we need to learn how to get our people to think as they worship. This will involve aspects such as: the selection of hymns/choruses on the basis of words as well as music; centring on a particular theme for the worship which relates to the preaching; brief introductory explanations to hymns, reading, prayers or other parts of the service. All these will be discussed in detail later.

All our strength

Fourthly, we are called to worship God with all our strength. This perhaps calls to mind our physical bodies and all our skills, talents and resources that are not included under the former three headings. It should also remind us that our body language is an integral part of worship. Physical touch, bodily movements, gestures and facial expressions are all used in our daily conversations with others and should be a vital part of our communication with God and the fellowship.

As we lead worship we need to be aware of our own body language – what we are saying without words. This should reinforce, not contradict, our spoken message. For example, if we are singing about God's overflowing joy in our life, we need to enter into the meaning and feeling of the song so that joy is evident on our face.[34]

At the same time we need to be alert to the people's sensory needs: sight, hearing, smell, touch, and taste – all these are relevant to worship. The celebration of the Lord's Supper is one example of a worship

---

[34] This may not be easy but it is important. However, it is vitally important that our worship and leading is genuine and does not become play-acting.

service that has tremendous potential as a rich sensory experience. Quite apart from any oral presentation or music, the service is full of visual imagery with the breaking of the one loaf[35] and the sharing of the one cup. There is bodily movement, the use of the senses of touch and taste as we share in the elements, the handshake of fellowship.

It is perhaps strange that whereas all churches universally celebrate the sacrament of the Lord's Supper or Holy Communion, rather few practise Jesus' injunction recorded by John from the same context:

> "Now that I, your Lord and Teacher, have washed your feet, you also should wash one another's feet. I have set you an example that you should do as I have done for you."   [John 13:14,15]

Foot washing is a remarkably powerful symbolic act when conducted in the context of worship. The action is a wonderful tactile experience, emphasising both the servanthood of the person washing the feet as well as the openness of the recipient to be served. The action can be fully inclusive, involving both congregation and leaders – all are called to servanthood.

More routinely, the worship leader should consider how bodily actions could reinforce worship. What actions are appropriate for praise, or confession, or prayer, or consecration? Particularly at what points the congregation should sit, or stand, or kneel, or move around the worship centre? When should our eyes be shut to exclude distractions or open to focus on an important visual part of the service?[36] How can our hands be used to give fresh emphasis to the meaning and feeling of worship?[37]

---

[35] In the letter to the church at Corinth Paul writes: 'Because there is one loaf, we, who are many, are one body, for we all partake of the one loaf.' [1 Cor 10:17]. This imagery or metaphor is largely lost by the use of wafers or by a 'crumbed' loaf.

[36] For example in the prayer of consecration of the bread and wine during the Holy Communion service it is probably more helpful to have ones eyes open so as to focus on the cup and the loaf held up symbolically by the priest or pastor.

[37] It is interesting that, whereas in modern worship styles raised hands are frequently used as a sign of praise, for the Hebrews raised hands were part of intercessory prayer. This is probably the meaning of 1 Tim 2:8 and is certainly what is depicted of Moses in Exodus 17:11. Possibly raised hands symbolically represent our life open (as a funnel) to receive God's blessing.

Principles

Are 'clap offerings' a legitimate part of contemporary worship or a reflection of secular concert or political culture?[38]

Worship also provides an opportunity to use our skills and talents to praise God. The people need to be encouraged to use their musical skills, their voices, their dramatic talent, and their reading ability in worship.

The Whole of Life

We have already discussed at some length in the opening chapter that worship is whole-life embracing, involving not only all that we are – our total personality – but also all that we possess, all that we do, all those to whom we relate. As such our worship services must touch and be touched by our daily lives and reflect faithfully our actual situation.

In practice this should mean confession that speaks to our faults and weaknesses, prayer that touches our concerns, preaching that understands our life situation and changes lives, praise and thanksgiving couched in terms that are relevant to the time and place in which we live. Much of the attraction of modern hymns is that the music is contextual and the lyrics drawn from everyday speech. By contrast, the rich language of 18th or 19th century hymns has a poetic feel but its meaning is probably largely lost on most of the congregation.

Whole-life embracing worship needs to address issues within the life of the church as well as wider society. If there are divisions within, worship should be a point for forgiveness and reconciliation. If there are tragedies affecting the community, nation or wider world, then worship should find expression for the sense of loss or outrage or concern. Worship should thus give us a God-context for understanding the world – an opportunity to understand God's view and to hear him speak and challenge our lives anew.

---

[38] Sometimes, for example, clapping would appear to be used in an ambiguous way as a response to hearing the Word preached. It is seldom entirely clear whether the preacher is being feted for an outstanding message or God is being honoured. In any case it is probably far more appropriate to have something that reinforces the message of the sermon or allows an appropriate response.

The Whole Worship Service

As already mentioned in the opening chapter, worship needs to be understood as referring to the whole worship service not merely the act of praising God. Thus the whole service needs to be planned as one integral act of worship that begins as the congregation gathers in prayerful anticipation and continues throughout the various acts and stages of worship. Through prayer, through song, through silence, through music, through confession, through praise and thanksgiving, through the giving of our offerings, through the reading of the Scriptures, through preaching, through the response to God's word, through dedication, through the final blessing – we bring our lives to God in a single act of worship, which, if we were to realise it, is just a short chapter within the book of worship – our biography.

Holistic worship means that the whole service must be understood as an act of worship. This is why casual conversation at points in the service, or indeed while we are preparing ourselves for worship, is so offensive to the very spirit of worship.[39] Whereas fellowship has its place within worship, this should not be an excuse for gossip and distracting chatter.[40] This of course applies to the worship leader too! All too often worship time is frittered away with idle comments about personal preferences, excuses for lack of preparation or elaboration of irrelevant or routine notices which everyone hears and ignores week after week!

The Whole Congregation

Worship is not about a leader, a music team or preacher giving a performance in the pulpit; it is about the whole congregation joining together in worship. The leader is there as an enabler, a conductor; not as an actor for an audience to respond to, but as someone who leads the

---

[39] The worship service is neither the time for the congregation to catch up on their weekly news, nor for the secretary to distribute letters, nor for the pastor to discuss forthcoming church activities.

[40] It may well be that if the congregation only meets once a week on Sunday that appropriate provision needs to be made for fellowship either before or after the service – perhaps with refreshments provided.

congregation into the presence of the King and enables them to respond to him in worship.

On occasions the worship is dominated by the worship leader, controlled by the music team or, in the context of contemporary British Methodism, monopolised by a one-man-band preacher.[41] This take-over of the worship is aided and abetted by the modern PA system that allows the leader, the singers or the musicians to completely overwhelm the worship, especially the singing.[42] It is also enhanced by a lack of flexibility or humility. For example, the author has experienced the leader of a worship team refusing to alter the prepared programme to permit a reading of the scriptures, as well as the preacher who publicly rejected the help of the person appointed to read the bible passage.

The concept of congregation as audience is not biblical. We are gathered together to engage in *corporate* worship. This means that every worshipper needs to be fully engaged and involved in the activity of worship and not sidelined on the touchline. We are not present to watch the match but to play in it! A fulfilling match is dominated neither by one player, nor the rules. So it is with worship. The liturgy, or the plan of the service[43], like match rules, is not the purpose of the game; rather it is a means of playing the game in an orderly fashion. Within truly corporate worship there should be many aspects where the congregation actively participate, rather than simply listen dumbly, and one suspects often mindlessly, to the leader. This involvement needs to be built into the structure of worship and may include activities such as: singing, responsive readings, prayer, testimony, reading of Scriptures, acts of fellowship and the like.

---

[41] This situation is now changing with the introduction of officially recognised 'Worship Leaders' who work alongside Local Preachers and Ministers in leading the worship.

[42] One good test is to stand outside the worship centre and listen to whose voice can be heard during the time of corporate singing. If it is the leader or 'back-up' singers only then there is something wrong.

[43] The usual criticism of liturgical worship is that it is rigid and fixed. However, most contemporary 'free' worship has its own pattern or order that is frequently no less rigid than a liturgy.

Then of course there is the matter of *inclusive* language. This has received more attention in the West partly because of the contribution of Christian feminists and partly because of the different nature of society. In Asia, Christians are largely content to use masculine terms in a generic way, as applying to the whole body of Christ, and are as yet generally untroubled by this issue.[44] However, in *all* contexts, there is a need to use language which embraces the whole congregation and the issue here is much wider than that raised by gender. One example of this is the use of the word *family*.

Frequently, in Britain, family is used to refer to the ideal nuclear family of two parents plus children. In this context we talk of 'Family Services'[45] and encourage families to sit together during the service. Beware! This usage can be very excluding for those who are not part of such ideal families, for example: the single-parent, the widow(er), the single, the separated, the divorced and of course children who are not accompanied by their parents.

The feelings engendered can be very powerful as I realised on one occasion whilst attending a Father's Day service, whilst 8,000 miles from home. During the service, all fathers present in the service were requested to stand. Subsequently the children of the church were given small presents to present to their fathers. It was an innovative idea, but unfortunately no one had taken account of the fact that one could be a father without having children in church to bring a gift! Similarly, Mother's day celebrations may evoke powerful emotions in the hearts of women who have never been able to have children.

The concept of family is an important one in the context of the church but it needs to be liberated from the narrow meaning of individual nuclear family to that of the 'Family of God' [Ephesians 2:19]. From this standpoint, a 'Family Service' is not about families, it is about the whole 'Family of God', which embraces every believer whatever their home situation, marital status, gender or age. Used in this light the term

---

[44] Languages such as Malay, or, spoken Chinese, in any case pose less of a problem as the masculine and feminine pronouns are identical.

[45] This is a worship service designed to be suitable for both adults and children. Sometimes referred to as 'All-age worship'.

Principles

is thoroughly inclusive and emphasises the relationship of the whole church as brothers and sisters in Christ and as sons and daughters of God.

There is also a need to be inclusive in our attitude to children. Frequently attitudes towards children are patronising or condescending. The church applauds their presentations and leaders refer to them as the future church. Equally, one could refer to elderly people as 'yesterday's church'. The essential point is that all are part of *today's* church! Children, teenagers, adults and the elderly are the church, the body of Christ. We need to recognise children's contribution to worship not as entertainment to be applauded but as something genuinely offered to God.

In summary, holistic worship only takes place where the whole congregation feels included and is swept up in the desire for, and activity of, worship. As leaders we need to inculcate into our congregations the longing to participate in and to prepare for a service, and lead in such a way that enables them to do so.

The Whole Godhead

Finally, in this chapter, there are two aspects that can be thought of under the heading of trinitarian. Firstly, the very nature of God. As we worship there needs to be a completeness in our focus upon God himself. On the one hand, we need to be aware of the majesty, the power, the holiness of our creator God, a remembrance which will inevitably cause us face our creatureliness, our sin, our weakness, our shortcomings, our dependence on His grace. Yet, on the other hand, the vision of the omnipotent King, the Lord God Almighty, needs to be held in tension with an awareness of God as our Heavenly Father – the one who loves, cares and provides for us his children. We need too, to meet God in Jesus, recognising that as we come together in His name, as his body, so he is present in our worship, as our Head.

Consequently, as we approach God in worship, we are first overcome in awe and wonder at His holiness, as was Isaiah[46]. But as we continue to

---

[46] Isaiah 6:1-7

worship, we become enthralled by the love, intimacy and communion that comes through his presence with us and the recognition of our new relationship with him. All this takes place through God the Holy Spirit who both leads us to a recognition of his holiness[47] and so pours his love into our hearts that we are freed to call God, "Abba, Father"[48]. Thus in our worship we focus on God the Father, through God the Son, led, guided and inspired by God the Holy Spirit.

There is, however, a second trinity of which we need to be aware. This is the inter-relationship in worship between the leader, the congregation and God Himself. It is not enough for the leader to lead; there must be a sense of anticipation and participation by the congregation, as well as the transforming presence of the Spirit, who breathes life into our worship and touches and changes our lives. Much of the direction and efficacy of our worship is determined on our knees, both as leaders and as the worshipping people of God. As leaders and preachers we need to teach our congregations the vital role they play in the development of *living worship*.

Summary

In summary, the concept of holistic worship emphasises the need to integrate our whole nature, our whole life, the whole worship service, the whole congregation, and the whole triune nature of God, into what we call worship. To neglect any of these aspects diminishes worship. Perhaps for those readers who regularly lead worship, now would be a good time to pause and consider how effectively your worship leading enables the whole congregation to worship God with all their heart, soul, mind and strength in a way that impacts their lives.

---

[47] John 16:8
[48] Romans 8:15

3 – Patterns

Worship as Relationship

Worship concerns relationships – our relationship with God and with one another in the family of God[1]. As we worship, we seek to develop these relationships: to know God, ourselves, and our brothers and sisters in Christ, in a more intimate and deeper way. Worship is of course a two-way relationship in which we must learn to both give and receive. To give love and receive love, to give to God and receive from Him, to give to our sister and receive from her. In worship we learn to open up the wholeness of our lives to God and to one another and sometimes this is a difficult and painful process.

If worship is about relationships, and Jesus certainly taught His disciples that His purpose in coming was to introduce them to their heavenly Father[2], then we should expect that our pattern of worship would include aspects which sought to develop and enhance this relationship. This is indeed the case, and so a basic pattern of Christian worship is modelled by relationship development. This is illustrated in the sections that follow.

Approaching God

Anyone who has experienced a noisy party will realise how difficult it is to get to know someone at a distance. We need to get close to them before we can enter into intimate relationship. Our life is a bit like a party – full of noise, activities, busyness and distractions that prevent us entering into a close relationship with God. This is the reason that many services begin with a 'call to worship' or a 'prayer of approach' intended to draw us into God's presence. This is a time when we

---

[1] The family (or, household) of God is one of the rich metaphors used to describe the relationship of believers to God and to one another. (Eph 2:19)

[2] John 14:6,7

quieten our hearts and minds and seek to leave behind worldly distractions and worries to focus on the Almighty ever-present God.[3] Thus James writes:

"Come near to God and He will come near to you" [James 4:8].

The Bible promise is sure: if we consciously seek God then he will be found by us. Or, in the risen Christ's words to the Laodicean Christians:

"Here I am! I stand at the door and knock. If anyone hears my voice and opens the door, I will come in and eat with him, and he with me."[4]

where Jesus promises intimate fellowship with those open to Him.

Thus at the beginning of a service a time of silence, a short prayer or collect[5], a verse of Scripture or a simple chorus[6] may provide the key for the worshipper to become overwhelmed by the reality of the presence of God. This time of drawing near should be an opportunity for awe and wonder – not extra time for latecomers to take their seats![7]

Whereas it is true that God is *Emmanuel*, always here with us, wherever we are, nevertheless our Sunday worship provides a special opportunity for enjoying God's presence, for being refreshed and strengthened by His life-giving Spirit. Our corporate worship mirrors the pattern of the Jewish Sabbath when all routine tasks and distractions are put aside to focus upon God Himself.[8]

---

[3] In some services leaders begin the service by an invitation to the Holy Spirit to come. This is perhaps a mistaken emphasis because the Holy Spirit indwells us and long before Pentecost the psalmist recognised the impossibility of running from the presence of God (Psalm 139:7-12). God is with us; what is necessary is that we realise it! It is we who approach God by setting aside the things that distract us and by opening our lives to him (Ps 109:23,34).

[4] Rev 3:20

[5] Collect is the term used to describe the short prayers prepared for different occasions and usually used in conjunction with liturgical worship.

[6] For example, a suitable chorus might be: 'Be still and know that I am God.', *Songs of Fellowship* No. 41.

[7] Late arrival of worshippers is very distracting and destroys the complete pattern of worship. This is a problem that should be addressed and overcome.

[8] Note, Sunday is the first day of the week and not the Jewish Sabbath which starts at nightfall on Friday until dusk on Saturday. Sunday became the primary day of Christian worship in celebration of Christ's resurrection that took place on the first day of the week (John 20:1).

Patterns

Removing Barriers

Sometimes our relationships with other people are spoilt by something that we have said or done, perhaps on some other occasion, even many years before. When we meet we feel awkward, we may try and avoid the other's company or there may be an uneasy silence. Such a breakdown in relationships is explicit in the hurting child's retort to a playmate:

> "I shan't friend you anymore!"

Unless the barriers are brought down by a frank apology or a making-up the relationship can never develop or grow.

In the same way, as we approach God, so we become conscious of all that hinders our relationship – the things we have done wrong, in thought, word or deed, or the things that we have neglected to do. These form barriers that need to be torn down afresh each time that we worship together. The apostle John puts the matter very bluntly:

> "If we claim to have fellowship with him yet walk in the darkness, we lie and do not live by the truth."[9]

In other words our sin and rebellion shut us off from intimacy with God, disrupting our relationship with Him. But there is a way of escape. Thus John continues:

> "If we confess our sins, he is faithful and just and will forgive us our sins and purify us from all unrighteousness."[10]

Barriers are brought crashing down as we acknowledge and confess our sin and seek God's forgiveness and cleansing.[11]

However, although all sin is against God[12], some actions or words also disrupt the fellowship in which we worship. Thus Jesus drew attention to the priority of restored relationships in his teaching about worship:

---

[9] 1 John 1:6

[10] 1 John 1:9

[11] This is perhaps a weakness in some charismatic worship that avoids the confession of personal sin and attributes the barriers that hinder our worship to the impersonal forces of evil that need to be bound and expelled from the worship place. In so doing there is a tendency to neglect personal responsibility for sin and hence the need for personal confession and forgiveness.

"Therefore, if you are offering your gift at the altar and there remember that your brother has something against you, leave your gift there in front of the altar. First go and be reconciled to your brother; then come and offer your gift."[13]

Reconciliation with our brothers and sisters must also be a part of the process of removing hindrances to worship.

Thus removing barriers speaks of confession and the assurance of forgiveness. It has to do with a sincere opening up of our lives to God for his examination, a praying together of the words of the psalmist:

"Search me, O God, and know my heart; test me and know my anxious thoughts. See if there is any offensive way in me, and lead me in the way everlasting."[14]

But we must not forget too it is about saying sorry to our neighbour, making up, and restoring the harmony of the fellowship. Our Sunday worship is never divorced from our everyday living and this includes the area of relationships.

Expressing Our Love

If we live in a close and intimate relationship with another, whether as parent, or child or spouse, at some point we will want to show our love. When the barriers[15] are removed and we can express what we really feel then a simple hug or a whispered 'I love you' will speak volumes.

Similarly, as we become conscious of the magnitude of God's forgiving grace and his love poured out upon us, even while we were enemies[16], so our hearts in turn are warmed and we long to reciprocate that love. We seek to declare his glory[17] and to become more aware of who He is and why He is worthy of our worship. As we praise, so we are swept

---

[12] Psalm 51:4

[13] Matthew 5:23,24

[14] Psalm 139:23,24

[15] Just as in worship so in our everyday relationships there are barriers that inhibit us. Sometimes it is the barrier of broken relationships – unforgiveness; sometimes it may be busyness, tiredness or preoccupation with worries.

[16] Romans 5:8-10

[17] Psalm 96:3, 1 Peter 2:9

along in a rising tide of adoration, supported by, and supporting in turn, other members of the congregation. We declare to God and to others that he is our Lord and worthy of our praise.

Thankfulness

One of the marks of healthy relationships is that people appreciate one another and express gratitude. A mother thanks a child for helping, a husband thanks his wife for preparing a meal, a boss thanks his employee for a job well done, we thank a stranger for her courtesy – all these build and strengthen relationships.

So it is in worship that we thank God. We bring to mind His continual care, protection and supply of our needs[18] and we give thanks. We realise afresh the miracle of life, health and strength and we give thanks. We acknowledge the special relationship we have with Him as our loving Father and we give thanks. We become aware of answered prayer and we give thanks. As we give our offerings we are reminded that all things come from God[19] and we give thanks.

Our songs and prayers of thanksgiving build and strengthen our relationship with God. We learn to trust him and see his hand at work in the detail and wonder of our daily lives.

Asking

In mature relationships, whether in the home, at school or at work, we are not afraid to ask – to ask for help or assistance, to ask for clarification, to ask for something that we need. If we are afraid to ask, or too embarrassed or too proud, then there is something wrong in the way we relate to others or they to us.

If we have the confidence to ask our parents for something then, even more so, we should be prepared to ask our heavenly Father, who longs to give us good things.[20] In a worship service our requests to God are usually referred to as intercession or petition. These requests need to be

---

[18] Psalm 46:1, Matthew 6:25-33.

[19] 1 Chronicles 29:12-14

[20] Matthew 7:11

rooted in thanksgiving[21] since our confidence to ask God is based upon the character of God and his past goodness to us. Underlying all our requests should be the desire to see 'God's Kingdom come' and a willingness to seek and accept his will for our lives.[22] Our longing for answered prayer should centre not on personal gain but a desire to see God's name praised and glorified.

Speaking

Although body language can be extremely informative[23], we normally build our relationships and knowledge of a third party through speech – through words. For example, every time we meet someone and greet him or her this strengthens our relationship.

In the New Testament Jesus is referred to as the Word of God[24] because God the Father makes himself known or speaks to us through the Son.[25] We also refer to the Bible as the Word of God because through it God still speaks to us in the 21st Century. As we meet in worship so God speaks to us – His word is declared. People act as channels or mouthpieces for God to speak to us. Usually, this will be through the reading of the Scriptures, or through preaching, although sometimes the Lord may speak through testimony, or prophecy[26] or interpreted tongues.[27]

---

[21] 1 Timothy 2:1

[22] Matthew 6:9,10

[23] In the field of counselling, body language, facial expressions and posture can be extremely revealing of feelings and what is going on inside the client. Indeed, a person's body language may be more truthful than his speech.

[24] John 1:1ff

[25] Hebrews 1:1,2

[26] 1 Cor.14:1-5

[27] It is the author's view that preaching should be the normal form of prophetic ministry, although this may not always be the case. Thus for example, Jesus was undeniably a prophet, yet Matthew summarises his ministry as one of: "...teaching in their synagogues, preaching the good news of the kingdom and healing...." [Matthew 9:35] There is no mention of a separate prophetic ministry.

Patterns

Listening and Learning

A major cause of breakdown in relationships is that the two parties have stopped listening to each other. Alternatively, some have never learnt to listen in the first place. It is a common human failing that we are usually so busy thinking what we want to say that we don't actually listen to our friend or partner. Or sometimes we may clock the words but not 'hear' the feeling or emotion with which they are charged. Suppose someone suddenly said to you: "It is finished!" His or her meaning needs to be interpreted according to the circumstances of the conversation but also by the depth of feeling accompanying the statement. It could mean the job or the crossword is completed; it could mean that your relationship was over; it could mean that the other party was suicidal!

Jesus pinpointed this problem amongst his hearers with the unusual challenge: "He who has ears, let him hear!"[28] He wanted them to really listen – not just mechanically to allow the words to filter through their consciousness but to engage with their meaning and respond to their demands. As leaders and worshippers alike we need to learn to listen to what God is saying if we really desire to grow in our relationship with him.

There are perhaps two keys to good listening. Firstly, we need to be silent. This is something we all find very difficult to do – not least in a worship service. Often we are so busy talking to God (singing his praises) that we have no time to hear him speak to us. Our worship must include quietness. The second key is a positive attitude. Someone once said he had never heard a bad sermon. That comment is illuminating because, I suspect, it tells us more about the listener than the quality of the preaching: how we need to cultivate an attitude of listening which enables us to hear the voice of God, if necessary, despite the preacher! We should constantly be asking ourselves not "What is wrong with this?" but "What has God to say to me?" Of course this applies not just to the preaching but the whole worship service.

---

[28] One example of many is Matthew 11:15.

Fellowship

Relationships inevitably involve having something in common. In a business relationship we have a common objective of making a profit; as parents we work together to build a home; as members of a football team we aim to beat the opposition. Indeed, unless we have some common aim or purpose or interest it is most unlikely that our relationship will grow and prosper.

In the New Testament the Greek word[29] that is translated as 'fellowship' has the basic meaning of sharing together in something with somebody. The word is used to describe the relationship we have with one another as Christians[30] as well as the relationship we have with God.[31] We worship together as members of one family – brothers and sisters together in Christ. We also have fellowship with God through his Son Jesus[32], and mediated by the Spirit[33].

This participatory relationship needs to be recognised and celebrated in our worship. Fellowship is perhaps most clearly focussed in sacramental services such as the Lord's Supper[34] or in baptism. In the communion service the one loaf[35] symbolises our essential unity as members of the body of Christ. Similarly, within the Baptism service, we welcome the baptismal candidate into the fellowship of the Family of God. More than that, the congregation may make a specific commitment of support as illustrated in the following liturgy[36]:

Pastor: *Members of the body of Christ, we rejoice that these, our sisters and brothers, have been baptized. Will you so maintain the Church's life of worship and service that they may grow in grace and in the knowledge and love of God and of his Son Jesus Christ our Lord?*

People: **With God's help we will.**

---

[29] *Koinonia*
[30] See for example Acts 2:42
[31] See for example 1 John 1:6,7
[32] 1 Cor 1:9
[33] 2 Cor 13:14
[34] Also referred to as Holy Communion or the Eucharist.
[35] 1 Cor 10:17
[36] The Methodist Worship Book, p 86

However, even within the usual weekly service there still needs to be some recognition of our relationship with one another and an expression of our love and care for each other. We will return to this later.

Commitment

Any meaningful relationship involves commitment. The marriage relationship is perhaps the best example. A man and a woman make a life-long exclusive commitment to one another. At the marriage service this commitment is declared in the vows, symbolised with a ring and attested by signature in front of witnesses. Although we formally give ourselves to our spouse at the wedding ceremony, that is just the beginning of a new and intimate relationship. It is a relationship that is continually built and strengthened, as we express our love by word and prove it by our actions!

Although we give ourselves to God primarily when we first accept His lordship of our lives at the point of becoming a Christian, yet nevertheless, we need to continually reaffirm our commitment to Him. In the context of worship our giving of offerings may be used as an expression of our love for the Lord and to symbolise the offering of ourselves in His service. Alternatively, depending on the challenge of the message, it may be appropriate to enact some demonstration of response to God's word.[37]

Blessing

Finally the ideal relationship is one that is self-enriching. As two meet together, not only are their individual needs met but the relationship itself is strengthened. As a consequence there is a sense of anticipation and eagerness each time they meet.

Worship, and I take this to include the preaching ministry, should be a channel for blessing, for healing and strengthening. Whereas there is sometimes criticism of those who go to Sunday worship for their weekly 'shot in the arm' or 'recharge of the batteries', surely there is something sadly wrong if worship is not a transforming experience. Certainly, we should continually draw on the Holy Spirit's power in our

---

[37] For example moving forward for prayer at the front of the church.

daily lives, but there is something special and empowering about corporate worship. We may receive the Lord's touch in different ways: conviction through the preaching of the Word; renewed wholeness through receiving the elements of bread and wine; healing and empowering through the laying-on of hands and prayer ministry. In a sense the means of grace are less important than that grace is received and that our lives are slowly but surely being changed into His likeness.[38]

The Structure of the Worship Service

In the first part of this chapter we have tried to picture worship as relationship. As we worship God so we enter into relationship with him. Just as our personal relationships grow and progress in stages, so too there is a sense of direction and progression within worship. This is enshrined in the structure of the worship service. To this we now turn.

Most services have a definite structure. Whereas this is clearly defined in liturgical worship, it is frequently apparent also in so called 'free' worship. There are several reasons for having structure. The first is encountered in Paul's letter to the Christians in Corinth. The Corinthian worship had become chaotic and individualistic and so Paul needed to give some instructions to restore order, both in the celebration of the sacraments and the regular worship.[39] Paul summarised his instructions with the words:

"But everything should be done in a fitting and orderly way."[40]

However, in addition to providing order, structure also ensures balance in the content of worship and enables a sense of progression or direction in worship. Balance is important as otherwise worship may be dominated by a particular element such as praise, or preaching, or sacrament. Direction is important as our worship should be heading to a

---

[38] 2 Corinthians 3:18
[39] 1 Corinthians 11:17-34; 14:26-40
[40] 1 Corinthians 14:40

Patterns

climax that empowers the worshipper to return to the world, and not wandering in unending circles from which the worshippers have to make their escape.[41]

It is important to note that order is not synonymous with a formal liturgy, nor does it prevent spontaneity and life within worship. Rather it provides a framework in which *living worship* can be expressed and created.

Orders of Worship

In some denominations the overall order of worship is prescribed in the form of a liturgy, but in many churches, especially independent or charismatic ones, there is no written form but rather the order follows some unwritten tradition.[42] Usually, formal liturgies have been carefully prepared before committing to print, and in this case the leader's main function is to work out how that liturgy can be most effectively used to create *living worship*. On the other hand, if there is no formal guide for the structure of the worship, the leader has a responsibility to plan an appropriate form that meets the needs of the worshipping congregation, is biblical[43] and balanced.

Worship orders are variable – there is no one single model that is suitable for all occasions. This is clearly evident in churches with liturgical worship where there are a range of services prepared for

---

[41] For example, sometimes if there is no liturgy there is no clear ending to the service and worshippers leave during the giving of the announcements or perhaps during a time of prayer ministry.

[42] In the author's experience, there are very few churches where the order varies dramatically from week to week. Even churches that pride themselves on spontaneity and being 'led by the Spirit' are surprisingly conservative when it comes to departing from the usual order. None of us starts the service from scratch except in cases such as the Pentecost experience (Acts 2) when the ground rules were completely changed!

[43] It is exceedingly difficult to lead sacramental worship adequately without any form of liturgy. For example, in a baptismal service, what are the questions to be posed to the candidates before baptism – if any? Should one baptise in the name of Jesus or the Trinity? What is the role of the congregation? What is the meaning of baptism? All these questions need to be answered in the course of the worship.

different occasions: Sunday worship, sacramental worship[44], and special occasions such as weddings, funerals, commissioning and so on. The same will be broadly true of 'free worship', although with perhaps less variety. In every case the worship must be appropriate to fit the needs of the occasion.

To understand how structures work it is helpful to look at some examples. The following is a general order of service that is based on the understanding developed earlier in this chapter on worship as relationship:

Entering God's presence
Approaching God
Confession
Assurance of Forgiveness

Enjoying God's presence
Thanksgiving
Praise
Offering
Intercession

Listening to God
The Word of God

Responding to God and one another
Response to the Word
Fellowship
Commitment

God's Empowering
Blessing

The service begins with the worshippers being brought into the presence of a holy God. The barriers of personal sin that hinder our worship are recognised, acknowledged and purged. This leads the worshipper to enjoy God's presence with thanksgiving for his grace, and praise for his character. The worshipper is then led to offer his gifts

---

[44] In Protestant churches two sacraments are recognised – baptism and Holy Communion. However, the Roman Catholic Church recognises 7 sacraments.

Patterns

as a practical token of that praise and thanksgiving. Inspired by the character of God, the worshippers are moved to intercede for themselves, the church, the community, the nation, and the world.

The intercessory prayer – speaking to God – leads on to listening to God through hearing the Scriptures read and the Word preached. God's Word demands a response from the hearer that may lead to practical expressions of fellowship, to renewed commitment and commissioning for further service in the world.

The order illustrated above is of course only the skeleton of the service which will be brought alive and transformed when the various ingredients of worship are added. However, the importance of establishing an order lies in ensuring that all the important aspects of worship are present[45] and that there is a natural connection between the various parts of the service. There are of course many possible variations. The alternative shown below is built on four main sections rather than five[46]:

The Preparation
Prayers of approach
Adoration
The Ministry of the Word
Scripture readings
Sermon
The Response
Confession
Peace
Offering
Thanksgiving
Intercession
Dismissal
Blessing

---

[45] For example, it is not uncommon to attend 'free' worship where there is no confession, intercession, Bible readings or thanksgiving. Note: both the orders of worship illustrated refer to non-sacramental services.

[46] This example is a summarised version of the 'Second Service' taken from *The Methodist Worship Book*, pp 39-50. By contrast Lutheran worship emphasises 3 main sections: 'Entrance', 'The Word', and '*Koinonia*' (fellowship).

The heart of this service is the preaching of the word. Thus, the first part of the worship is understood as a *preparation* to listen to the word, and the subsequent worship is seen as a *response*. Similarly, confession is seen as a consequence of preaching rather than a preparation for worship. Furthermore, the offering, thanksgiving and intercessions follow on the hearing of God's word. The element of praise finds emphasis throughout the service.

In contemporary charismatic worship in non-liturgical churches the structure of the worship is less clear cut but usually consists of three main sections: Praise, Preaching and Prayer ministry. The first section, often labelled 'Praise and Worship', is designed to carry the worshipper into the presence of God as well as act as a preparation for preaching. It may or may not have an element of confession. The prayer ministry is designed to allow a two-way response to the word – the worshipper actively seeks God's blessing and God touches, heals, gives new life, and equips through that prayer.

Having adopted an overall order, the art of worship preparation revolves around choosing the basic ingredients that will most effectively implement the different aspects of worship. These ingredients will be discussed shortly. There is also a need to decide how much time will be assigned to each aspect of the worship. For example, the section of praise might take the form of just a hymn or prayer of praise or, alternatively, might involve a corporate time of adoration and praise lasting 30 minutes or more. Similarly, the preaching might be a 10 min sermonette or a whole hour Bible exposition. The choice is usually guided by the 'tradition' of the church involved or the special needs of the occasion.

The Flow of Worship

One of the most important aspects to understand about preparing an order of worship is to take note of the progression of ideas within worship and to see how one aspect leads naturally to the next. Worship, like a sermon, should have direction or aim and be moving slowly but surely to a climax. Not only this, but the worship should flow, one part merging into the next without unnecessary interruption or distraction. Much of the art of worship leading is knowing how to link one part with another. A parallel is perhaps a film editor, joining different parts of film so as to make one seamless whole.

The ever-present danger is that worship can become like commercial TV with continuous advertising breaks, especially at the high points! Very often the continuity of worship is broken by the felt need to always introduce personalities who are taking part in leading, singing, reading, preaching, giving notices and so on. Our task as worship leaders is to introduce our congregation to our Lord and not to continuously interrupt this process by screening credits for the various participants.

For the service to flow, not only do the various parts need to be linked but also the participants in leading the worship have to be ready on cue. A few examples to illustrate this are as follows. The starting of the service should not be delayed because of last minute testing of microphones or adjusting of the music group's amplifiers or tuning of instruments. Similarly, the Scripture reader should be ready in place to read at the close of a hymn or prayer and hence does not interrupt the flow of worship by walking the length of the church while the congregation wait. The Sunday School children are ready to move to the front to give their presentation immediately they are invited to participate. In worship, every moment is precious and not to be wasted.

The Ingredients of Worship

Whereas the order of worship is basic to planning a worship service, the ingredients actually used to implement the order determine the final service. For example, a given order can become a fairly formal worship, suitable for an aging, traditionally minded congregation, or interpreted in a style in which young people or the most charismatic would feel at home. The atmosphere or flavour of the service is largely dependent on the ingredients, the style of leading and the degree of corporate involvement of the congregation.

As we go on to think in more detail about the worship service, it is helpful to consider some of the various ingredients that may be involved. However, it is important to recognise that worship is more than the sum of the ingredients of a worship service. Just as the ingredients of a cake when baked in an oven become a whole new reality, so it should be with worship. In both cases the actual product is dependent on the ingredients and how they are put together. Even with one basic recipe – a formal liturgy – it is still possible to create a variety of end products by the judicious choice of the variable ingredients. Some of these are now briefly discussed.

Song

Much of contemporary worship is sung. This is of course not limited to traditional hymns or modern worship choruses. There is opportunity to sing the psalms or scriptures or responses set to music, formal prayers (such as the Lord's prayer), *Taize* chants and, within charismatic worship, the beautiful experience of singing in tongues. Perhaps because worship preparation is not taken sufficiently seriously these aspects are rarely explored to their full. Most worship runs in a rut of 'the same as usual', and few worship leaders, whether leading liturgical or free worship, take the trouble to be innovative.

A further weakness is the use of songs that do not fit the context. For example, in Asia, the vast majority of worship songs or hymns are still Western in origin, sung either in original languages or translation. As a consequence the worship is not contextual and neither touches the heart nor feeds the understanding[47]. A song or hymn written in the local context using local music and local rhythms speaks much more powerfully to the people than those that are foreign to their experience. This principle is true the world over.

Variety is one of the keys to *living worship*. The Lord's Prayer, which is routinely said Sunday by Sunday, may become a vain repetition. But set the same words to music and the congregation can focus on the meaning in a new way. It comes alive, at least for a while. Similarly, many worship leaders who lead the congregation in a prolonged period of chorus singing, often use a very restricted corpus of songs. As a

---

[47] Consider, for example, the line of a hymn: 'God does not promise skies always blue …' In Britain a blue sky with its accompanying sunny weather is a constant hope. In many other countries, including the tropics, constant blue skies means a drought – hot unbearable weather and a water shortage. Quite the opposite meaning!

consequence the worship slips into a routine of familiarity that is no different to the repetition of set prayers.

There is of course a further possibility for diversity – the singer. The congregation can be taught or instructed to sing in parts. There can be a choral item (whether by a regular choir or group of Sunday School children etc.) or perhaps even a solo. However, the aim must always be clear. It is so the congregation can more adequately worship – not so they can be entertained!

Music

Apart from accompanying or leading singing[48], music has a role in its own right as an ingredient of worship. There can be music before the worship to help create an atmosphere in which the congregation can prepare themselves. Music can also make a very effective background for various aspects of worship such as: a dramatic reading of Scripture; a time of quiet meditation; an opportunity for personal praise; an accompaniment to the giving of offerings; a link between different parts of the service. Although some aspects can be scripted and pre-planned, much is dependent on the sensitivity of the organist, pianist or music team.

Further variety can be derived from the musicians themselves. Increasingly today, worship is being accompanied by a wide spectrum of instruments in addition to the more traditional organ or piano. This is potentially refreshing, but the musicians need to learn to work together as a team. An important aspect of this is a willingness both to play and remain silent. Much contemporary accompaniment is spoilt by the apparent desire of all the musicians to play all of the time, and as loud as possible – with modern amplification systems this can be a painful

---

[48] It is interesting to contrast styles between the more traditional worship accompanied by piano or organ and the contemporary music team. The role of the worship leader in the former style of worship is to introduce or announce the hymn and then the musical lead-in is given by the piano or organ. The advantage of this is that the worship leader does not need to have an outstanding singing voice. By contrast, in much contemporary worship the musical accompaniment provides an indistinct lead and it depends on the worship leader to lead-in the singing. This inevitably restricts worship leaders to those who have outstanding musical skills.

experience for worshippers! On occasions the unaccompanied voice of the congregation is very uplifting.[49]

Even in a small group, with little or no musical talent, one should not despair. In Sunday School, children can often provide a very helpful accompaniment with simple homemade instruments (such as rice-shakers) or a tambourine. As a last resort you can use a tape-recorder, if necessary finding someone who can play the tunes for you to record.

Silence

Perhaps this is one of the most neglected ingredients of worship. It has much to do, no doubt, with our 21st Century lifestyle where we find it difficult to be still or quiet even for a few moments. At home, there is often the ceaseless background noise of the TV or radio or CD player. In church, there is so often the continual chatter of the adults or the noise of the children. We need to rediscover the art of silence, of being still. The psalmist encourages us to be still before God with the words:

> "Be still and know that I am God; I will be exalted among the nations, I will be exalted in the earth...."[50]

Although the actual context of the preceding text is that the Lord calls the warring nations to cease their furious activities and be still before the Lord their creator, the verse is surely relevant to worship. We are called to cease from our hectic activity of the week to be still in the presence of the Lord.

'Being still' is of course more than not making a noise or moving around. It refers to an inner stillness of the soul focussed on the presence of God; to the inner quiet, the sense of harmony and

---

[49] For example, on one occasion I attended a renewal meeting with maybe a thousand people present. During the first part of the evening a competent music team with a full complement of singers led the worship. The worship was good. In the middle of the message the preacher decided he wanted the congregation to sing a particular song but the worship team had already dispersed to their seats in the auditorium. We sang unaccompanied and it was heavenly. For the first time that night I could hear the congregation as opposed to the 'singers' worshipping!

[50] Psalm 46:10

peacefulness of the heart centred upon God[51]; to the calmness that quietens our fears and enables us to wait for God to answer our needs[52]. Being still is of course not only a discipline to be learnt but is dependent upon having the time to do so. This surely is part of the blessing of the Sabbath[53] ordinance that one day a week we should pause from our round of continual activity to be still before God.

We need to learn for ourselves how to be quiet before the Lord, how to wait for Him, how to shut out the distractions that crowd in upon us and focus our full attention on His presence. We also need to teach our congregations this secret and provide a worship service with space to allow it to happen. A worship service that has no opportunity for quietness lacks an important dimension.

The Spoken Word

Many aspects of worship involve the spoken word. On the one hand, there are the contributions of individuals – leader, preacher or member. This may include: reading the scriptures, preaching, prophecy, prayer, drama, giving testimony, announcing the notices and introductions to different parts of the service. On the other hand, there are corporate activities in which the whole congregation is involved and this may involve: prayer, liturgical responses, reading the Scriptures or affirming a creed. It is important that there is a right balance between corporate and leader oriented activities so that the congregation is not left as spectators.

It is also important that attention is given to excellence in presentation so that the congregation can be encouraged and so that members can

---

[51] Isaiah 26:3

[52] Psalm 37:7

[53] The Sabbath ordinance appears as the fourth of the 10 commandments (Ex 20:8-11) that commands us to observe one day in seven as a 'holy' day, a day to rest from our work and focus on God. Christians no longer celebrate the Jewish Sabbath, Friday night to Saturday afternoon, but assign Sunday, the day of Christ's resurrection, as the day for worship and rest.

hear the introductions, be challenged by the reading of the Scriptures[54] and can understand the notices.

Visual Elements

We live in a visual age and through TV, video and computer games we have become addicted to visual stimuli. Consequently the visual aspects of worship are of fundamental importance in our whole worship experience. Historically the Roman and Orthodox churches have placed much more importance on the visual and dramatic aspects of worship than the Protestant churches with their unadorned buildings. Whereas one might question the theological significance of elaborate vestments and richly adorned altars with their plethora of candles and worship accessories, yet one cannot deny they do have an attraction to the worshipper. Why? Because they are visual! They are symbols that convey the wonder and mystery of worship more effectively than the spoken word.

Slowly, particularly under the influence of the Charismatic movement, Protestant churches are rediscovering the art of the visual. In addition to the ubiquitous OHP, or nowadays the computer-interfaced LCD projector, churches are becoming decorated with texts and banners, and worship is accompanied by dance – a highly visual art form, perhaps not so remote as some might like to think from the elaborate drama enacted by the priest in some Catholic and High Anglican traditions.

But of course there is much more. Even without the addition of vestments, sacramental services such as the Lord's Supper or Baptism are highly visual and dramatic. Sadly, much of the rich symbolism is lost because of a preference for convenient communion elements – crumbs, wafers or slices of bread – rather than the one loaf[55]. Again many communicants have never been taught to feast their eyes on the rich visual spectacle, and so have their eyes closed in prayer when they

---

[54] Reading the Scriptures is not just a matter of putting someone on the rota but also providing training, advanced notice of the passages and opportunities to practice and be given feedback. This is discussed in more detail in Ch 5.

[55] In Asia a variety of Indian 'breads' are closer to the reality of the unleavened bread of the Jewish Passover meal and can easily be 'broken' and distributed.

Patterns

should be observing the drama of the Last Supper re-enacted for them. Much more attention needs to be given to visual ingredients.

The use of the OHP and similar multi-media equipment is almost completely unexplored apart from providing the words of songs. It can be used for sermon illustrations, for shadow plays, for giving notices, for illustrating prayer. In addition to the OHP, there is of course the slide projector which can be used to bring powerfully visual images to aid our prayer, whether intercession or thanksgiving. Or perhaps a video clip projected using a LCD projector.[56] Our use of visual stimulation needs to go beyond artistically arranged flowers, to consider the whole decor of the worship place. Is it a place of joy, light and warmth, or a place of shadows, darkness and cold? Our worship place needs to be attractive so that people will want to come to worship, and having come, be aided in that worship.

Movement

Closely related to, and indeed overlapping with, the visual, is the aspect of movement, but in this case we are concerned more with the participation of the worshipper than what is seen. On the whole, in traditional liturgical worship, the movement of the congregation has been heavily circumscribed, restricted mainly to standing, sitting and kneeling. The Charismatic renewal has transformed this situation and opened up the congregation's involvement in worship through more expressive body movements. These include aspects such as: clapping, raising hands and dance as an aid to praising God. Then there are prayer walks, extending the hands in prayer, laying-on of hands[57] in intercession and prayer ministry. Processions to worship or within the body of the Church[58], moving to the front to receive the sacraments or

---

[56] Some aspects of the use of multi-media are discussed in a book on alternative worship by Draper and Draper (2000) pp 36-44.

[57] Laying-on of hands in prayer-ministry may be controversial in some traditions as it is normally used exclusively for confirmation and ordination but it appears to have been used by Jesus in blessing children (Mark 10:16).

[58] For example, in one Roman Catholic church in Sabah the Sunday School children line up outside the church before the service. As the service begins the children process into the body of the church and then out through a side door for their Sunday School class. The whole designed to remind the congregation that the children are part of the Church.

prayer ministry, or to give one's offering, all these involve movement. Body language is also encountered in more formal liturgical settings, for example, shaking hands as worshippers 'Pass the Peace'.

Body language is a very important reinforcement of oral statements and actions have a powerful affect on the participants. They are particularly helpful in releasing the more emotive aspects of worship and lifting songs of praise beyond just the mind. As always there is a need for balance and perspective and to realise that the attitude of kneeling before God in worship can be just as expressive as standing and vice-versa.

Summary

It is hoped that this chapter will have opened the reader's understanding to grasp something of the scope of worship in terms of the various aspects, ingredients and structures. In the light of this it should begin to dawn on the reader that preparing for worship leading is time-consuming. In my experience, thorough worship preparation can take as long as preparing a sermon. Only thorough preparation will lead to *living worship*!

4 - Prayer

Prayer should permeate the whole of our worship and indeed our daily lives as Christians. Through prayer we reach out to God and in turn are touched by His presence. Many Christians find prayer difficult in their daily lives and consequently struggle in praying openly with others or leading prayer within worship. Leading prayer is not simply knowing techniques of praying but rather it is an extension of our individual and corporate prayer lives. Prayer is never simply saying words; it is expressing our earnest desires and feelings towards God; it is offering our lives and all that we hold dear to God; it is longing to know his plan and purpose; it is a desire to enter into intimacy with God. As we lead others in prayer, so our own lives are challenged and changed.

Facets of Prayer

There are many facets of prayer but the simple acrostic **ACTS** summarises four aspects which should always be present in our own prayer life and in worship.

>A is for *adoration* or praise, and denotes that dimension of prayer which concentrates on who God is and expresses our recognition of His worthiness.

>C is for *confession*. This is our response to the holiness and majesty of God as we recognise that we fall short of His glory, and that our lives need cleansing from sin.

>T is for *thanksgiving*, that is, our response to what God has done, is doing, and will do, for others and us. Through thanksgiving we express our gratitude for God's blessings, especially His love shown to us through the life, death and resurrection of Jesus.

>S stands for *supplication* or intercession and reminds us that God is our Heavenly Father who longs to hear and answer our prayers. Through our intercessions we bring to God the needs that we perceive in our own lives, the life of the church, community, nation and world.

It needs to be emphasised that all true prayer is theocentric, that is, centred on God. Even within our prayers of intercession we need to learn to pray: "Thy Kingdom come, thy will be done...", as Jesus himself taught the disciples.[1]

Whereas it is possible to identify other aspects of prayer that are encountered within worship, many of them may be included under the four main headings given above. For example, invocation or 'drawing near' to God is a prelude to adoration. Likewise, prayers of dedication or commitment may be an extension of confession, since as we confess our sin to God we will wish to rededicate our lives to Him and to seek His renewal and empowering. Offering prayers are often very akin to prayers of thanksgiving. The blessing is, in many ways, a prayer of intercession in which we claim God's goodness to overshadow the assembled congregation.

Ways of Praying Together

As a worship leader our brief is not to pray for, or on behalf of, our congregation, although we may well do that in private. Rather, our task is to lead the congregation to pray. This means that our public prayer should never take the form of a soliloquy, or an overheard conversation with God, that is, we are not inviting the congregation to be an audience to our private prayer with God. We should pray in such a way that the congregation can understand and identify with the prayers and enter together with us into the presence of the King.

This must mean that the form our prayers take should encourage a sense of corporate involvement. At the very minimum, we need to pray aloud in such a way that the congregation can make sense of our leading and endorse the prayer, making it their own, perhaps with an audible Amen!

It should be appreciated that there are many different ways of praying together. Effective inclusive worship will often use a variety of different forms appropriate to both the congregation and that part of the

---

[1] Mat 6:10

worship service where the prayer occurs. Some of these forms of prayer are outlined below.

Extempore Prayer

This is a form of prayer, used by many worship leaders, where the prayer is spoken out loud but not from a script. This form of prayer develops naturally from participation in prayer groups, where members get used to praying aloud as though conversing with God. Such prayer is relevant to most aspects of worship and can be used equally for: adoration, thanksgiving, confession and supplication. The advantage of this form of prayer is that it can be spontaneous, adapted to the moment and fresh. The disadvantages are that it requires a degree of experience and confidence; it may easily become exclusive, especially in long prayers, to the point that the congregation may not feel involved and become marginalized; it may be limited in scope, repetitious or irrelevant.

One way of avoiding the last set of disadvantages is to have an outline for the prayer. For example, in a prayer of praise the leader might note down the characteristics of God that are praise-worthy and will form the basis of the prayer. In the case of prayers of intercession the leader may record the topics or persons to be prayed for. Extempore prayers are probably best, at least in the early days of worship leading, for short times of prayer such as may accompany the dedication of the offering or mark the beginning of the service. Extempore prayers should never be used as a substitute for preparation.

Written Prayers

Written prayers may take two forms – either prayers written by the worship leader or prayers obtained from other sources. Both are very valuable. Although writing one's own prayers is very time-consuming, nevertheless it is very important since it enables one to address specific situations and also to reflect thoughtfully on the substance of the prayer. The use of prayers written by others is very helpful since it provides access to a whole wealth of Christian tradition and experience. Often the beauty of written prayers can be very uplifting.

Written prayers can be drawn from a wide variety of sources that include: collections of prayers, the Scriptures, and service or prayer books[2]. Service books often contain a variety of prayers, including short prayers or collects[3], suitable for the various occasions of the Church year. A specific example of a collect, which is normally used at the beginning of a service, is as follows:

> Almighty God, to whom all hearts are open, all desires known,
> and from whom no secrets are hidden: cleanse the thoughts
> of our hearts by the inspiration of your Holy Spirit, that we may perfectly
> love you, and worthily magnify your holy Name;
> through Christ our Lord. Amen

Written prayers can be used in different ways. On occasions the congregation may be given the words (in a service book, the Bible, or on a notice sheet) and can pray together with the leader. On other occasions the leader will 'read' the prayer. The leader should take care to be familiar with the prayer and pray in such a way that the people are unaware that there is a script[4].

Litanies

A variation on the theme of a written prayer is a litany. This takes the form of a series of short statements by the leader with a response by the congregation. This would normally be fully scripted. A biblical example of a litany is seen in Psalm 136 – a short section[5] of which is given on the following page:

---

[2] Two particularly helpful resources are: *Patterns for Worship* (1995) and *The Methodist Worship Book* (1999).

[3] Collect is the special name given to short prayers used in liturgical traditions. The prayers, dating back to at least the seventh century, are usually a single sentence in length and are normally used at the beginning of a service and are often preceded by a time of silent reflection.

[4] This occurs when the leader has adequately prepared and is genuinely praying the prayer rather than simply reading the words on a page. The leader needs to experience the prayer and communicate that experience to the congregation. Only in this way will the prayer come alive.

[5] Psalm 136:1-5 (CEV)

Prayer

> *Praise the LORD! He is good.*
> **God's love never fails.**
> *Praise the God of all gods.*
> **God's love never fails.**
> *Praise the Lord of lords.*
> **God's love never fails.**
> *Only God works great miracles.*
> **God's love never fails.**
> *With wisdom he made the sky.*
> **God's love never fails.**

The congregational response is the uniform 'God's love never fails'.

Litanies may of course have a variety of congregational responses that are appropriate to the theme of the prayer. For example, litanies are suitable as prayers of praise, thanksgiving, confession or intercession. The advantage of litanies is that they encourage corporate participation; the disadvantage is time-consuming preparation.

Responsive Prayers

Another approach is to use short (simple enough to be memorised) or well-known responses. For example:

Intercessions:
> Leader: *Lord hear our prayer.*
> People: **And let our cry come to you!**

Confession:
> Leader: *For all our sinful ways.*
> People: **Father, forgive!**

Praise:
> Leader: *For great is the Lord!*
> People: **And greatly to be praised!**

Thanksgiving:
> Leader: *Give thanks to the Lord!*
> People: **For He is good!**

The responses, which can be used in a variety of ways, could be included on a notice sheet or displayed using an OHP.

One approach, for intercessory prayer, is to state a particular concern or need for prayer, then allow a time of silence for people to pray and afterwards conclude with a response. This pattern can then be repeated several times. Thus in a period of intercessory prayer the leader might begin:

> Let us now pray for those who are sick or suffering at this time. (*pause*) We remember especially ... (*names*) ... and others known to us. (*Pause*) We pray for the Lord's healing hand to touch them. (*Pause*) We pray for peace instead of pain. (*Time of extended silence.*)
>
> Leader: *Lord in your mercy.*
> People: **Hear our prayer!**

This pattern is then repeated with the second and subsequent items of intercessory prayer until the leader concludes the prayers with a simple prayer such as:

> Loving Father, we bring to you our prayers for ourselves and for others. We come in confidence, asking that Your will may be done and Your Kingdom come. In Jesus' Name. **Amen**

Open Prayer

'Open prayer' provides an opportunity for individual members of the congregation to lead in praying aloud. On the surface this may seem to be the easiest form of prayer as it apparently requires little preparation. In fact it is probably the most difficult, especially where the congregation is not used to this way of praying. For open prayer to be a helpful experience precise instructions are vital since the congregation must know exactly what is required of them. For example, the following instructions might be given:

> 1. We are now going to have a time of open prayer where members of the congregation are invited to lead us in prayer.
>
> 2. In our prayers we are going to give thanks to God for all the blessings showered upon us as individuals, as a church, as a community and as a nation.
>
> 3. Prayers should be short and to the point so that several people can lead us in prayer.
>
> 4. Let us pray together.

Prayer

After several people have prayed the leader will draw the time of prayer to a close.

The normal pattern of open prayer will consist of:
- Instructions.
- Short and simple introductory prayer by leader.
- Period of quiet in which people have an opportunity to pray.
- A closing prayer.

This type of prayer works most effectively with small congregations[6] and with groups who are used to this pattern. It needs to be introduced carefully so as not to give the congregation a bad experience.

The biggest difficulty is to encourage participation. The starting point is to create the right atmosphere for prayer. If the theme of the session is praise, then singing an appropriate chorus of praise or adoration may be helpful *after* giving the instructions for the prayer time. The leader's relationship with the congregation is also vital – if the leader is physically distant from the congregation, and is using a microphone, then it is difficult to provide an informal and conducive atmosphere. There is much to be said for the leader joining the body of the congregation and leading without amplification for this part of the service.

Another practical aid is to ask a few people before the service to be ready to pray aloud so as to catalyse the session. The leader might also suggest the people use a verse of scripture or a hymn as the basis of their prayer. This is often very reassuring for worshippers who are not used to praying aloud in front of the whole congregation.

Yet another means of encouraging participation is to use open prayer together with a response. For example, if the focus of the prayers is praise, then the following response could be used after each prayer:

> Leader: *For great is the Lord!*
> People: **And greatly to be praised!**

Such a response frees people to pray aloud.

---

[6] In large groups the individual voice can rarely be heard unless there is provision of mobile microphones or the people come to the front to use a fixed microphone.

Open prayer may often be blended with songs of praise and adoration. A musician sensitive to the atmosphere may begin playing the melody of a well-known chorus, prompting the congregation to sing. Alternatively, a member of the congregation might initiate the singing.

The leader's role in open prayer is crucial. Sensitivity to the congregation and the atmosphere is vital so that the session is introduced and concluded in an appropriate way. It is particularly important to judge the right length for the prayer time and to conclude in a way that acknowledges the prayers of the whole congregation in a positive way. Possible words to conclude a time of praise, which acknowledges both the spoken and silent prayers, are as follows:

> Almighty and ever-living God, we offer to you our prayers of praise, both those spoken out loud and those uttered in the quietness of our hearts. May our lips and our lives ever continue to praise you without ceasing. In Jesus' Name we pray. **Amen**

With One Voice

A variant of open prayer that is widely used in Asia is praying with one voice. In this form of prayer everyone participates and prays out loud at the same time. Often people may be praying in different languages and of course this also gives opportunity for worshippers to use the gift of praying in tongues without distracting others. This may take some time to get used to but it does provide an opportunity for everyone to be involved. The leader will bring the time of prayer to a close when a suitable period of time has elapsed.

The advantage of this type of prayer is that it is suitable for all sizes of congregation from small groups to huge celebrations. The leader, especially if using a microphone, must be sensitive when leading such prayer, otherwise the leader's voice dominates, which is very distracting for individuals trying to pray. After inviting the people to pray 'with one voice' the leader should pray quietly, allowing the people's voice to be heard. The prayer time is brought to a close as the 'voice of prayer' quietens down.

As a preliminary to prayer the leader should provide the focus of prayer – whether intercessory or praise or thanksgiving. Sometimes the prayer may be enacted in waves – a prayer item is announced, the people pray, the prayer quietens and then another prayer item is announced and the people pray again. Finally the leader ends with a suitable concluding prayer.

Traditional Prayers

There are a number of written prayers with a long tradition of use as congregational prayers. Such prayers are normally memorised by the congregation and may be either prayed together or sometimes sung. These include: the Lord's Prayer, the Grace, the Doxology, and various choruses or verses of hymns that might be used as prayers.

Whereas there is always the danger that familiarity breeds contempt, nevertheless, these well known prayers are very important as they are thoroughly corporate and carry with them a long tradition of Christian worship going back to the time of Jesus[7]. Furthermore, they provide a link between Christians from different denominations and church background and are a unifying tie with our brothers and sisters in Christ throughout the world. Prayers that are committed to memory are especially helpful for those who are illiterate or partially sighted. This, of course, includes young children who often feel excluded from worship because there is so little with which they can be involved. Note, these prayers can be used to draw together a period of prayer or even to conclude a service or a fellowship group meeting.

These prayers can, of course, be used in a variety of ways. For example, the words of the Grace:

> The grace of our Lord Jesus Christ,
> and the love of God,
> and the fellowship of the Holy Spirit
> be with us for evermore. Amen.

are appropriate to conclude a prayer session or to close a service or a meeting. The prayer may be said in unison and may be used as a prayer

---

[7] Of course, very many of these prayers are derived from the Scriptures, for example: the Lord's Prayer (Mat 6:9-13) and the Grace (2 Cor 13:14) and thus cannot be dismissed as mere tradition as they provide a living continuity with the Early Church community.

of blessing on one another. Sometimes it may be effective to pray with eyes open, looking around at fellow members of the congregation as we bless them.

Similarly, the Lord's Prayer can be prayed in a variety of ways so as to bring the prayer alive. The prayer can be sung, said together with pauses at appropriate points for reflection, or prayed responsively[8] as follows:

Our Father in Heaven,	Hallowed be your Name
Your kingdom come	Your will be done
On earth	As in heaven
Give us today	Our daily bread
Forgive us our sins	As we forgive those who sin against us
Save us from the time of trial	And deliver us from evil
For the Kingdom	The power
And the glory	Are yours
Now	And forever. **Amen.**

Furthermore, the Lord's Prayer can be used at a variety of points in a worship service. For example, it could be used at the conclusion of a time of confession, using an introduction such as:

> As forgiven members of God's family let us say together (or, responsively) the prayer that Christ has taught us. ... Our Father ...

Alternatively, the prayer could be used to conclude prayers of intercessions as follows:

> Let us offer to God our prayers of intercession by saying together the Lord's Prayer. ... Our Father ...

Inviting Prayer Topics

Another way of increasing the participatory nature of prayer is to invite the congregation to suggest prayer topics and then use them to form the basis for your own extempore prayer. This is appropriate for prayers of intercession, praise or thanksgiving. There is, however, one Golden

---

[8] The responses can be alternated between leader and people, men and women or two halves of the congregation.

Prayer

Rule – if you invite prayer topics you *must* use or acknowledge the suggestions in some way in your prayer.

Invited prayers are especially helpful in the informal atmosphere of a Family Service[9], but remember to take children seriously and do *not* laugh at their suggestions or encourage the congregation to do so. If a young child asks prayer for a sick pet, that is a sincere[10] request and should be taken seriously – we should not forget that Jesus taught that God cares for all His creation, even the birds of the air[11]. It is helpful to actually write down the requests so that none are forgotten or overlooked[12].

Praying in Groups

Although this is perhaps unusual within a worship service, it can be employed with great effect. The leader introduces the time of prayer and asks the congregation to divide into small groups of three or four in order to pray together. Depending on seating, it may be easier to stand together to pray rather than to try and sit together in a group.

One helpful variant is the 3 **N** format where each member of the group is asked to share: their *Name*; some *News* about themselves; and a prayer *Need*. After sharing, the group prays around the circle, each praying for their neighbour. Finally, the worship leader draws to a close the prayer time by uniting the congregation in a known prayer such as the Lord's Prayer.

Care must be taken to avoid embarrassing individuals, especially any who may not be Christians. If there are likely to be non-Christians

---

[9] Here 'Family Service' refers to a service for the whole 'Family of the church' that includes children, youth, adults and the elderly and not to a 'service for families' where singles and the elderly may feel left out.

[10] Of course you may encounter a child or teenager who tries to embarrass the leader or disrupt the service by making some spurious suggestion. However, with quick thinking almost everything can be turned into a suitable subject for prayer, even if you end up praying for football players or the influence of TV programmes.

[11] Mat 6:26

[12] Some churches use an 'Intercessions' book where members can write down prayer needs. This can then be incorporated into the intercessory prayer time.

present, the leader can encourage them to be open about their situation in the group – and of course they would not be expected to pray.

A particular advantage of prayer groups is that it involves everyone – even children or elderly people can take part. At the same time it promotes interaction and mixing between members of the congregation, especially if the leader encourages people to group together with others whom they do not know. Furthermore, prayer groups on a Sunday probably involve far more people in prayer than all the prayer fellowship meetings during the week.

Listening to God in silence

Most of us live busy, noisy, non-stop lives and the very idea of silence or stillness is often strange or even threatening to us. However, silence is vitally important if we are going to explore the full depths of prayer. Prayer can never be reduced to reading God a 'shopping list' of requests or reciting a list of his attributes. In prayer we come into the presence of God and open up our hearts, our minds, and our souls to Him. Silence is an important part of prayer as it permits us to listen to God.

Silence involves being still – not just our bodies and our tongues but still within. We need time to be quiet, to calm ourselves, to become aware of God's presence. Silence also involves focus. Without a focus we become distracted and stray thoughts will carry us away from God. The focus might be a word or a verse of scripture or it might be an object – a stone, a candle, a cross, a picture, the bread and wine at a sacramental service[13]. The focus could also be our lives – our past, our present, or our future – examined before God.

Silence in corporate worship also requires a quiet atmosphere in the worship centre. If people are talking or babies crying or there is traffic noise or loud music, it is probably best to avoid any pretence of silent prayer.

If silence is a new experience for the congregation, then the leader needs to clearly explain what is about to take place and how to *use* the

---

[13] Sometimes to actually handle – touch, feel, smell or taste – can aid our focus.

Prayer

silence. It is important that the congregation realise that silence is not just the absence of noise or waiting for the next item – it is a positive time to be used. Having created the appropriate peaceful atmosphere and having explained the purpose of the silence, the leader needs to introduce the focus. The focus could be meditative as in centring on the flame of a candle; or introspective as we listen to God's personal challenge on our lives; or intercessory as we concentrate on lifting someone to God's healing touch.

Times of silence are particularly appropriate during a Holy Communion service[14], after hearing the Word read or preached, in intercessory prayer or at the end of a service. Normally the time of silence will have been very carefully planned and prepared, but just sometimes the Holy Spirit may so touch the congregation that silence in awe and wonder is the appropriate, spontaneous response. At such moments God indeed renders us speechless.

Prayer Ministry

In corporate worship most prayer is focussed on and involves the whole body of Christ. However, in every service there will be individuals who have particular needs that are not adequately addressed in the general prayer. These may be needs that have been brought with the worshipper to church, such as ill health, worry, fear, or failure. Alternatively, the needs may be a response to the worship or preaching – faith in Christ, a recommitment to discipleship, a desire to be spiritually equipped for God's service, a longing to know more of God. In each case it is helpful if there are opportunities for prayer ministry[15].

The way in which prayer ministry is handled will depend on the discipline or practice of the church. Some common approaches include the following:

> ➢ Personal prayer at the communion rail whilst receiving the sacrament.

---

[14] For example, for the purpose of self-examination or meditation on the wonder of Christ's sacrifice or the unity of the Body of Christ.

[15] Prayer ministry refers to specific prayer by the preacher, pastor or other appointed leaders relating to personal needs.

- Personal prayer at the front of the church following an 'altar call'.
- Personal prayer after the church service has concluded.

The church leadership needs to discuss and agree how such prayer should be conducted, especially: i) Who should pray? ii) Where and when should the prayer be ministered? iii) How should the prayer be conducted?[16]

The worship leader needs to pay attention to several issues. Firstly, the agreed practice of the church should be followed. Secondly, the invitation for prayer ministry should be clear – who is invited, for what purpose, when and where. Thirdly, the leader should make it easy for people to respond to the invitation – possibly invite the congregation to stand and sing an appropriate song while people come to the front[17]. Fourthly, the leaders or team should be invited to come forward to assist in the prayer ministry. Lastly, the congregation should be clear as to their role – are they to continue worshipping in song, or to join in general prayer for those at the front of the church?

It is very important, especially if a large number of people come forward, that there is still a definite end to the service, that is, that the congregation doesn't slowly disperse while the prayer ministry is being continued.

Prayer ministry can be a very enriching experience that tries to take seriously scriptural injunctions concerning prayer[18]. Whereas such ministry can take place in private in a home, there is something particularly empowering about prayer in the context of corporate worship. It does, however, need to be planned. Firstly, who is to minister? Is it just the preacher, the worship leader, or a ministry team? Remember if only one person is praying for individuals then the process may be quite time consuming, maybe thirty minutes or more.

---

[16] For example, some churches conduct prayer ministry with laying-on of hands whereas others reserve this form of prayer for the bishop at confirmation or ordination services.

[17] It is very difficult to come to the front if everyone else is sitting, watching.

[18] James 5:13-16

Prayer

What is the congregation supposed to be doing[19] whilst prayer ministry is going on? Clear instructions must be given and provisions made. How is the corporate worship going to end? Will there be opportunity for testimony, or did the service end when people were invited for prayer ministry?

An alternative to public prayer ministry is to invite those who have come forward to stay behind or to move into a side room after the service. One advantage of this approach is that the ministry can be less rushed, and it is perhaps easier to arrange follow-up. This latter point is very important as frequently those who come forward for prayer may need further counselling or therapy to deal with long term emotional problems, or practical help with an ongoing difficulty, or nurture as a new Christian.

Prayer in Action

In chapter two the importance of the whole person in worship was emphasised. Involving the body or actions in our prayer is part of that concern. It includes, of course, how we pray – do we kneel, sit, stand or walk? Do we put our hands together or do we raise our hands[20] in intercessory prayer? Do we have our eyes closed, perhaps to exclude distractions, or do we focus on some object in our prayer?

But prayer in action is more than just the attitude in which we pray; it involves actions that become part of our prayers. Walking forward to the front of the church in response to an altar call is already a prayer in action. In the very act of moving to the front we are seeking God's blessing on our lives.

Action prayers can be particularly helpful in confession of sin or in consecration of our lives to God. For example, the congregation can be encouraged to write down the sin that they want to confess to God and subsequently come forward and nail[21] it to a specially prepared wooden

---

[19] The people might continue in worship, singing appropriate quiet songs, or they may be invited to continue in prayer for those who have gone to the front.

[20] This is the Jewish tradition in intercession as in Moses' prayer. (Ex 17:10-13)

[21] One can, of course, stick the papers onto a cross, but the act of 'nailing' the sins as Christ was nailed is particularly moving.

cross[22]. Alternatively, the confessions can be placed on an offering plate and subsequently publicly burnt to denote that they have been forgiven and are no longer counted by God.[23] Or, in a small group, the members could symbolically draw their sin on a white board and subsequently all the symbols of sin are erased and the board wiped clean with an appropriate reading of scriptures.

Action prayers are very helpful in consecrating our lives in God's service. For example, if the sermon has focussed on the story of the young lad's gift of loaves and fish,[24] the challenge might be for the congregation to offer something to Christ. The people can be given small pieces of card shaped as a loaf or fish and write their offering on the card. Afterwards it can be offered together with their financial gifts as a prayer of commitment. Other examples of action prayers are suggested in a helpful book on prayer in worship.[25]

Closing Prayers

The beginning and ending of services are crucial. Often the first or last aspect is prayer. This should be carefully chosen. It is often appropriate to close with a well-known prayer such as a collect or blessing. Many of these prayers are derived from the Scriptures[26], and a few examples are given below:

> The Lord bless you and keep you;
> the Lord make his face to shine on you and be gracious to you;
> the Lord look on you with kindness and give you peace. Amen.[27]

or,

> The blessing of God, the Father, the Son and the Holy Spirit
> remain with you always. **Amen.**

These prayers may be made inclusive rather than priestly by substituting the word us for you.

---

[22] Afterwards the leader or pastor must take care that the papers are destroyed or burnt.

[23] Psalm 103:12

[24] John 6:9

[25] Webster (1994) p 40-41

[26] See, for example: 2 Cor 13:14; Jude 24,25; Phil 4:7.

[27] Numbers 6:24-26

Prayer

Alternatively, the service might end with a prayer of dismissal such as:

> Leader: *Go in peace in the power of the Spirit*
> *to live and work to God's praise and glory.*
>
> People: **Thanks be to God. Amen.**

Or, by the congregation saying 'The Peace' to one another or in response to the leader:

> Leader: *The peace of the Lord be always with you.*
>
> People: **And also with you.**

Leading Prayer

So far we have concentrated on the various ways of praying. In drawing this chapter to a close it is important to make one or two comments that specifically relate to leading prayer.

Many leaders when they begin leading prayer unconsciously speak more quietly – perhaps as an act of reverence to God. However, it is important to avoid this. Leaders need to speak up and use a volume similar to normal leading; otherwise people will not hear. For the same reason, it is important not to drop your voice when introducing prayer. The invitation: 'Let us pray', should be spoken boldly and clearly so that all can hear. (It is perhaps instructive to reflect that frequently the best compliment given by those who minister in Old People's Homes is not that the message or worship is good, but that the residents can hear!) Beautiful prayers are valueless if the worshippers cannot hear what is said.

In leading well-known prayers, for example, the Lord's Prayer, it is important to continue to give an audible lead as this helps to keep the congregation together in the prayer. The leader's voice should set the speed that should be slow enough for people to realise what they are saying. Ensure that you have a copy of the words to hand. A well-known prayer may suddenly be forgotten in front of a crowd of people.

Leaders often find it difficult to judge times of silence. A few minutes of quiet can seem like eternity when standing in front. Usually inexperienced leaders allow too short a time and tend to rush from one part of the prayer to the next. It is important to allow the congregation to take in what is being prayed about before moving on.

Prayers should be brought decisively to a close with a well-known formula such as: 'In Jesus' Name' and a clear distinct 'Amen' that the congregation affirm. This applies especially to periods of open prayer whose end should be clearly demarcated to prevent confusion.

Finally, the leader needs to be thorough in preparation of prayer before the service, but also to be ready to include additional aspects of prayer, especially items for intercession that may arise. For example, if a child or other member of the congregation is celebrating a birthday or special anniversary, then be prepared to pray for them – especially if the birthday is publicly acknowledged. Similarly, be ready to pray for people moving away from the church or students going to university.

More practical hints about leading in general, many of which are relevant to prayer, will be dealt with in a later chapter.

Summary

Prayer is a vital part of the Christian life and of worship. All the different aspects of prayer: adoration, confession, thanksgiving and supplication have a place in our corporate worship. There are a wide variety of ways of leading prayer in worship that are appropriate for different points in the service. The worship leader can helpfully introduce a range of styles so as bring new life to the people's prayer ministry and thus help to create *living worship*.

5 - Preaching

At first sight it might appear odd to have a chapter entitled 'Preaching' in a book on leading worship, but in reality preaching and worship are inseparable. Preaching nearly always takes place in the context of worship, and worship itself is incomplete without the proclamation of the Word of God. In some church traditions this relationship is well understood and the preaching is dovetailed into the worship service – the worship prepares people to hear the Word, and the preaching inspires worship. In much contemporary worship this relationship is less well understood and frequently the worship and preaching appear to be running on different tracks with no clear relationship.

If the relationship of worship and preaching is recognised, then the worship leader and preacher will work together in planning and preparation. How this is done is discussed in the paragraphs that follow.

The Christian Year

One of the obvious links between worship and preaching is the Church or Christian Year[1]. The Church Year is in essence a celebration of the life, ministry and saving acts of Christ that takes place throughout the calendar year. The purpose of the Church Year is to proclaim, commemorate and explain the Gospel through both worship and preaching. It also functions as a focus of unity for Christians throughout the world who celebrate the major festivals at the same time.

Whereas readers from a liturgical tradition are probably familiar with the Church Year, others may have only a rather hazy understanding and so an abbreviated form is summarised on the following page. It is probably helpful to make one or two general observations. Firstly, apart from Christmas Day, all the celebrations are moveable – the dates being

---

[1] A more detailed discussion of the Church Year is available in White (1990) pp 72-87

Season/ Celebration	Period/ Date	Purpose/ Theme
Advent	4 weeks – starting end of November	Christ's first and second comings – thanksgiving and anticipation.
Christmas	2 weeks	The Incarnation
Christmas Day	December 25th	Celebration of Christ's birth
Epiphany	About 8 weeks starting January 6th	God manifest in Christ – Christ's baptism/ Signs and wonders.
Transfiguration	Last Sunday	The glory of Christ revealed
Lent	40 weekdays (March/ April)	Fasting – preparation for Easter. Jesus' wilderness experience, ministry and final journey.
Ash Wednesday	First day of Lent	Repentance
Passion Sunday	2 weeks before Easter	The suffering of Christ
Palm Sunday	The Sunday before Easter	Christ's triumphal entry into Jerusalem
Maundy Thursday	Thursday before Easter	The Last Supper, Gethsemane, betrayal, arrest and trial
Good Friday	Friday before Easter	The Crucifixion – death of Christ
Easter	Seven weeks	
Easter Sunday	Variable date March 23rd to April 25th	The resurrection of Christ
Ascension Day	The 6th Thursday after Easter	The ascension of Christ
Pentecost	About 25 weeks	Celebration of the coming of the Holy Spirit/ Birth of the Church
Pentecost Sunday	7 weeks after Easter	The coming of the Holy Spirit
Trinity Sunday	Sunday after Pentecost	Celebration of the Trinity

Preaching

fixed each year by reference to the Jewish festivals, specifically the date of *Passover* which is determined from a lunar calendar.

The Eastern Orthodox Church celebrates Epiphany (January 6th) rather than Christmas and various cults and sects reject the celebration of Christmas completely[2]. It will be also noted that some celebrations of the Church Year take place on weekdays as well as Sundays. In the early Church the Christians worshipped daily[3], but eventually Sunday rather than the Jewish Sabbath became the main focus for worship. The main reason for this is that the 'first day of the week' became special as a celebration of Christ's resurrection. Thus every Sunday, worship is a mini-Easter celebration.

The observant reader will notice that whereas the Lenten season is celebrated over a period of more than 6 weeks, the actual number of days assigned to this period is only forty. This period is chosen to parallel Jesus' forty days wilderness experience[4]. The two periods can be reconciled when it is realised that the six Sundays in Lent are excluded from the fasting period.

Apart from the main festivals summarised in the table, individual churches may include their own special Sundays or celebrations. For example, often special days are set aside for: harvest festivals[5],

---

[2] For example, the Jehovah's Witnesses and Seventh Day Adventists reject Christmas on the basis that it is a pagan festival. Historically, the celebration of Christ's birth on December 25th started after the conversion of the Roman emperor Constantine at the beginning of the 4th Century AD. During his reign the traditional pagan festival which took place at the winter equinox in celebration of the 'Sun god' was replaced by commemoration of the birth of Christ. Christmas is not a pagan festival but the Christian festival that replaced it. It is unlikely that December 25th accurately reflects the birth date of Christ which is generally thought to be around Springtime in the Western hemisphere (March-April). Practically, it would be difficult to celebrate both Christ's birth and death at the same time and so the retention of December 25th as the date for celebration of Christ's birth is meaningful.

[3] Acts 2:46.

[4] Luke 4:1-13

[5] It is of course not sensible to have a fixed date for the worldwide church since harvests occur at different times of the year in different parts of the world. For example, in Sabah, East Malaysia, the rice harvest is celebrated at the end of May, whereas in Britain the harvest festival will normally take place in late September.

thanksgiving (gift) days, mothers' or fathers' day, Remembrance day[6], Bible Sunday, Reformation Day and New Year's eve[7]. There may also be special days to focus on or remind people about: the church anniversary, missions, children and youth work, or social concern.

The importance of the Church Year is that it provides a coherent way of telling the Christian story throughout the year in a way that reinforces what we believe and provides opportunities for proclaiming these truths to others. Thus many outside the Church will have some awareness of major festivals such as Christmas and Easter and these provide opportunities for Christians to witness to their meaning[8].

Lectionary

The word lectionary comes from a Latin word meaning reading. It refers to a systematic way of reading the Scriptures in worship either on a daily or weekly basis[9]. The lectionary readings are related to the Church year so that the chosen passages reflect the main theme each Sunday. Normally, four readings are suggested for each service and these comprise:

- An Old Testament passage
- A Psalm
- A Gospel reading
- A New Testament reading (apart from the gospels)

Sometimes the psalm may be used as part of the liturgical worship rather than as a formal reading. In some church traditions there are only two readings, one from the Old Testament and one from the New but in

---

[6] This is a Sunday set aside to remember those who died during the World Wars and reflect on the horror of war and the cost of freedom.

[7] Of course in Asia the Church many not only celebrate the Western New Year but also other New Years, in particular Chinese New Year that generally falls around February in the Western calendar.

[8] Christmas and Easter are marvellous opportunities for explaining the wonder of God stepping into His world in Christ Jesus, and of God's love displayed in Christ's sacrificial death on the cross.

[9] This system is used especially by churches with a liturgical tradition such as: Anglicans, Lutherans and Methodists.

Preaching

other traditions, notably Anglican, both a gospel and epistle reading are normally included. The overall theme of the readings then becomes the basis for the preaching.

To show how it works, a set of the suggested passages for Christmas Day and Easter Sunday are provided below.

Christmas Day
- Isaiah 9:2-7 ('For to us a child is born...')
- Psalm 96 ('Declare his glory among the nations...')
- Luke 2:1-14 (Birth at Bethlehem/ the shepherds)
- Titus 2:11-14 ('The glorious appearing of our great God...')

The readings[10] have been selected to tell the Christmas story starting with the Old Testament prophecy from Isaiah of the coming child, through the Gospel account of the birth and angelic proclamation to the shepherds and ending with a Pauline reflection on the wonder and consequence of the incarnation.

Easter Sunday
- Isaiah 65:17-25 (A new hope a new future)
- Psalm 118:1-2, 14-24 (Victory – 'I will not die but live')
- John 20:1-18 (The empty tomb and appearance to Mary)
- 1 Cor 15:19-26 (The centrality of the resurrection)

The above readings have been picked to emphasise various aspects of the Easter message. In turn, the readings refer to: a radical new beginning; Christ's victory over death; the evidence of the empty tomb and His resurrection appearances; the centrality and significance of the resurrection in the Gospel proclamation.

Importance

The strength of the lectionary is that it provides a systematic way for reading the Scriptures in a worship service and provides balanced focus

---

[10] The readings are taken from the lectionary of the Methodist Church in Britain – Year C readings.

on the Old and New Testaments. It helps both preacher and worship leader to identify a theme and encourages the people to worship with their minds as well as their hearts.

Using the Church Year

It is clear that both preacher and worship leader can make good use of the Church Year in determining the shared theme of the worship and preaching. The Church Year can be used in a variety of ways. Some will use the lectionary with its prescribed readings to determine the theme of the message and the worship. The advantage of this discipline is that the preacher is encouraged to engage with Scripture rather than coming to the Bible for proof-texts to support preconceived ideas. The worship leader has the advantage of knowing the Bible readings in advance and has some idea of the theme that is to be engaged in the worship.

Without the framework of the lectionary, preacher and worship leader have to work much harder to ensure balance in worship and preaching and to faithfully interpret the Church Year. At its worst the Bible reading is neglected as an integral part of worship, the worship is monotonously similar from week to week[11] and the important themes of the Church Year are neglected or misinterpreted.

A particular example of the latter is a misunderstanding of the Easter story. On a number of occasions I have attended Good Friday services where the worship has centred on the victory of the cross and a celebration of Christ's triumph over death in the glory of the resurrection. No thought has been given to Christ's suffering, the meaning of His sacrificial death or the awfulness of sin which separates us from God. Conversely, I have attended Easter Sunday services where the prime focus has been on the cross and the death of Christ

---

[11] For example, in many non-liturgical services the main element of worship is praise. The main themes are rarely connected with the preaching and often focus on martial themes – God as mighty victor defeating the power of the evil one. Christians as the army of God who need to rise up in the power that God gives.

rather than a celebration of His resurrection[12]. Such confusion detracts from a clear proclamation of the Easter story.

If the lectionary is not used, then it is imperative that the pastor, the church leadership or those responsible for worship and preaching in the church, should plan a programme which at least takes account of the main festivals and seasons within the Church Year so as to guide preachers and worship leaders. These also need to be made known to the congregation, maybe through the church bulletin or weekly notices.

Connecting Worship and Preaching

We have seen that the Church Year can provide a connection between worship and preaching through identifying a specific theme for the service. In this section we are going to look at practical ways of making that connection.

A Common Theme

There are various ways of identifying the overall theme of a service. The theme may be determined by the Church Year, by a sermon topic or by the type of service – baptism, communion, wedding, funeral, evangelistic and so on. In each case the message and the components of worship should have some connection with the theme.

The Message

On occasions the theme of the service may be determined by the content of the message. For example, the message may seek to address practical or topical issues such as: prayer, giving, the gifts of the Spirit, evangelism, social concern or discipleship. The message apart these themes can be addressed through appropriate:

- ➢ Scripture readings
- ➢ Songs or hymns
- ➢ Prayers
- ➢ Special items such as drama, testimony and so on.

---

[12] For example, the worship leader picked the hymn *When I survey the wondrous cross...* rather than hymns celebrating the resurrection glory.

For example, if the theme of the service was 'prayer', then it would be appropriate to select Bible readings which focussed on prayer, examples of men and women of prayer or God's promises concerning prayer. Similarly, some of the songs or hymns might emphasise the importance of prayer or the effects of answered prayer. Even the times of prayer themselves might focus on prayer – confession for lack of seriousness in prayer; thanksgiving for answered prayer; intercession that the church might become a people of prayer.

The theme of prayer could also be addressed through a drama enacting God's people at prayer, such as the church in Acts, or a more modern example such as George Muller, or some contemporary scene. Apart from drama, members could be invited to share testimonies relating to their practice of prayer or to answered prayer. Finally the service might be brought to a close with God's people invited to be involved in intercessory prayer or to be prayed for in a time of prayer ministry.

The Service

On other occasions the type of service might determine the theme. For example, at a baptism service Bible readings will helpfully be related to examples of baptism in the Bible or texts that help in understanding the meaning of baptism. Songs and prayers can also touch on the theme of baptism or discipleship that follows on from baptism. There will also need to be some formal or informal liturgy[13] relating to the actual act of baptism that explains the meaning of the sacrament and enacts it in a Biblical way. It may be helpful to provide an opportunity for the new believer(s) to give a testimony and it may be appropriate for the congregation to pledge their support or to pray for those newly baptised.

---

[13] It is vitally important in a 'Free church' or 'Charismatic' tradition without a formal liturgy to prepare an adequate 'order of service' as well as wording for baptism. Thought should be given as to what is required of the candidate. Should he or she renounce past allegiances (sins) and publicly confess faith in Christ as Lord and Saviour (Rom 10:9). Into whose name is the new believer to be baptised – the Name of Jesus (Acts 2:38) or the name of the Father, the Son and the Holy Spirit (Mat 28:19)? Should prayer be made for the baptism of the Holy Spirit to accompany water baptism? And so on?

Preaching

A funeral service[14] or wake[15] will have totally different purposes and themes. These will include opportunities to grieve, to acknowledge the death of a loved one and to say 'goodbye' to the deceased. This may involve thanksgiving to God for the life of the deceased. The service will also provide comfort to the bereaved with a clear proclamation of the Christian hope that we have in Christ of eternal life that continues after death. It may also provide opportunity for the congregation to reflect on the meaning of life and death. All these themes have to be conveyed by appropriately chosen songs or hymns, prayers, readings and liturgy.

There are, of course, many other types of service with differing themes. In liturgical traditions the worship leader is aided in structuring the service by the given order. This, of course, has to be made relevant to the congregation by the appropriate choice of songs and hymns, readings and message. Leaders in congregations without liturgical guides could helpfully consult some modern liturgies[16] or orders of worship in preparation for such services.

Positioning The Sermon

We also need to think about the place of the sermon within the overall worship service. This is usually determined by the liturgy or the tradition of the church. But it need not be so! The positioning of the sermon should be determined by the inter-relationship of the preaching and worship. Three distinct understandings are summarised in the table on the following page.

The first pattern (**I**) understands worship as essentially preparing the congregation to hear the Word. Thus the message comes towards the end of the worship service that closes almost immediately after the message. In this way the application of the message is carried home with the congregation.

---

[14] For an excellent detailed discussion of conducting funeral services see Walter (1990).

[15] This term is used here to describe an informal service taking place usually in the home of the deceased to comfort and strengthen the family, and often in Asia to be an act of witness to the eternal hope that we have in Christ.

[16] Church of England (1995) and Methodist Church (1999) are helpful resources.

The second pattern (**II**), which is much less common, sees the proclamation of the Word as the inspiration for worship. The message is thus brought very close to the beginning of the service and is followed by the main body of worship. This may be the case in a sacramental service where the preaching of the Word precedes the celebration of the Lord's Supper or in a wedding ceremony where the message comes before the actual marriage rite. The early positioning of the message could also be appropriate if the application of the message demands it. For example, a sermon on worship or the God whom we worship might naturally lead to an extended time of worship in response to the message.

The positioning of the sermon in the worship service

No	Role of worship	Appropriate Order
I	Preparation	Worship *The Word* Close
II	Response	Introduction *The Word* Worship Close
III	Preparation and response	Worship *The Word* Worship Close

The third pattern (**III**) is also very helpful as it allows worship to both prepare people to hear God speaking to them and to give a response in worship. Of course, the content after the message will be very different from that which precedes it. The worship after the message will encourage and enable the congregation to make a response. It might be a hymn of consecration, a time of prayer ministry, an act of offering our

Preaching

gifts to God or possibly intercessory prayers. But each will be moulded so as to enhance rather than to detract from the effect of the message[17].

Preacher and Worship Leader in Partnership

In some traditions or situations one person will both lead the worship and preach. However, this section is intended for occasions when preacher and leader are different persons who need to work together. In the ideal situation the two persons will meet together to discuss, pray and plan some days before the worship service. Each has a distinct role and these are described briefly in the following paragraphs.

The Preacher's Role

The preacher is essentially responsible for deciding the overall theme of the service. The theme may be guided by the season of the Church Year, or the lectionary readings, or a topic suggested by the church leadership, or by prayerful consideration of the people's needs or in response to some major issue in the news[18]. In order to work effectively with the worship leader the general theme probably needs to be fixed a week before the service.

At the initial meeting with the worship leader, or over the phone, the preacher needs to provide the following information:

- The theme and aim of message
- Bible readings
- Particular hymns as preparation or response to the message
- Any special requirements – altar call/ visuals etc.
- Positioning of the sermon.

---

[17] Worship leaders should resist the temptation to summarise or repeat the main points of the sermon or, worse still, try to add to the sermon! One should also avoid encouraging the congregation to offer a 'clap offering' to God for the message. This is barely distinguishable from applauding the speaker and invariably distracts from the heart of the message. The role of the worship leader is to apply the message of the sermon through the worship so that it touches the heart, is memorable and is carried home with the people.

[18] For example, if a tragedy or horror of the magnitude of the 9/11 terrorist attacks in New York were to occur in the week preceding the service this would need to be addressed at some point in the message.

The preacher will normally arrive early before the service to check any special arrangements and to pray with the worship leader and the worship team. The preacher will pay particular attention to the pulpit and the timing of the sermon so that a smooth changeover can be made with the worship leader. It may be worth standing in the pulpit or the designated preaching place in order to check practical aspects such as sight lines and operation of microphones. As a preacher, I also find it particularly helpful to be in the pulpit during the hymn before the sermon so as to get a 'feel' of the congregation and to silently pray for them.

The Leader's Role

Whereas the preacher will provide the overall theme of the service, the leader will be responsible for the major content and the order of the service. Usually the worship leader will be part of the home team, whereas the preacher may be a visitor. Consequently it is the worship leader who will know the congregation and their worship experience and will be able to assist the preacher in choosing any special songs or arranging special items or facilities.

It is normally the worship leader's responsibility to make the initial contact with the preacher to confirm the theme, the readings and any particularly relevant songs or special requirements. The leader will also provide the preacher with any necessary practical advice concerning the use of pulpit or microphones. The leader will also co-ordinate with those responsible for reading the Bible passages, the musicians and any others involved in the practical running of the services.

The leader needs to ensure that the sermon fits seamlessly into the overall worship. In practice, this means ensuring that the preacher is ready in place to preach at the end of the previous worship item. Probably the smoothest hand-over will take place if a suitable hymn or song precedes the preaching[19]. During the singing, the preacher can go to the pulpit or take over the microphone from the worship leader. It is usually not necessary to introduce the speaker who will normally be

---

[19] The song might introduce the theme of the message or alternatively be in the form of a prayer asking that the God will prepare our hearts to listen to the Word.

Preaching

named in the church bulletin. If it is a special visitor, a few brief words of welcome and introduction can be given in the notices – if these are given earlier in the service – or before the hymn preceding the message. However, the leader should at all times draw attention to the message and not focus too much on the speaker.

After the message, the leader should move on smoothly to the next part of the worship service, where possible reinforcing the message of the sermon by applying it to what follows. One should avoid drawing attention to the speaker or distracting from the challenge of the message with comments such as:

> "We would like to thank Mr Brown for an outstanding message…"

or,

> "Let's give a clap-offering to God for a challenging sermon …"[20]

There is no need to comment on the message unless you can encourage the people to respond in the worship that follows.

In the event that the Lord has spoken powerfully through the preaching, there may be no need for words – the people may be moved to respond spontaneously. Sometimes, however, it may be helpful for the leader to encourage the people to make a specific response, for example, the leader might say:

> "I believe that the Lord has spoken powerfully to us through the message we have just heard. Let us continue in a time of silence, making our personal response to God."

or,

> "This morning the Lord has challenged us to offer the whole of our lives in His service. If the Lord has spoken to you this morning I would like to invite you to come and kneel at the front of the church as a practical token of your response."

Sensitivity to God and to the people is all-important. Without such sensitivity the people will not adequately respond to the message.

---

[20] This sounds spiritual but in reality tends to mimic secular applause. In any case, it 'closes' the message and does not permit continued application in the worship that follows.

Summary

Preaching and worship are intimately related. This relationship can be strengthened by a unified theme suggested perhaps by the Church Year or lectionary readings. Preacher and leader need to work together so that the worship both prepares the way for the message and provides an opportunity to apply the message to people's lives. Preaching, in turn, should inspire the people to worship, and challenge them to live their daily lives as an act of worship.

6 – Praise

In recent decades praise has been the main focus of worship, especially in churches influenced by charismatic renewal. So much so that, although praise is by no means the whole of worship, they have become inseparably linked together in people's thinking and vocabulary[1].

However, although praise has been in the forefront, its expression has been mainly limited to singing. This is seen both in liturgical and non-liturgical traditions. For example, in some Anglican churches, a time of praise (singing) is grafted on to the liturgy either as a preliminary to the main worship or as a section in its midst, whereas, in non-liturgical worship a time of praise in song may constitute nearly the whole of the worship, leaving little room for other elements.

Praise is undeniably central to worship, but urgent attention needs to be paid to the way in which we praise God, in particular to:

 ➢ Providing variety in our expressions of praise.
 ➢ Integrating praise into the overall pattern of worship.
 ➢ Having a balance between praise and other aspects of worship.

In this chapter we will begin to address some of these issues through examining biblical patterns of praise, and applying them to worship in today's Church.

Praise in the Scriptures

The word praise appears nearly 300 times in the NIV version of the Bible, the majority of times in reference to praising God, with most of these citations in the Old Testament.[2] It follows that the Old Testament texts, and especially the book of Psalms, largely guide our

---

[1] For example, worship leaders and contemporary books on worship frequently use the phrase 'praise and worship'.

[2] In the NIV version of the Bible there are 296 references to the word praise, 257 in the Old Testament. A small proportion refers to the praise of people.

understanding of praise[3]. In the paragraphs that follow we shall summarise some of the teaching of the Scriptures concerning praise, especially: the reasons for praise; biblical patterns for praising; and the relationship of praise and thanksgiving.

Praise and the Reasons for Praise

Praise, in essence, means to say something good about someone. In the context of worship it means to say something good about God. Other words that are sometimes used which have similar meaning are: bless, exalt, magnify, extol, glorify, honour, or acclaim. In the Bible, praise is given to God because of His essential character or nature and also because of His actions. Sometimes praise is linked together with thanksgiving, which has, however, a rather distinct meaning. Thanksgiving is an expression of gratitude for God's blessing, gift and help. Put succinctly, praise addresses who God is and what He does; thanksgiving focuses on how we personally benefit from God's actions or being.

God's Character

There are numerous references to praise focussed on the character of God. Some examples of these are shown in the table on the following page. This is not an exhaustive list of God's attributes but rather a selection of those that have motivated God's people to praise Him.

The list is rather arbitrarily divided into four sections which focus on: God as Lord, King, Creator and Redeemer or Saviour. Many of the attributes could variously be included under different heads. For example, whereas the attribute of 'power' is listed under God as Creator – with respect to His creative and sustaining power – it would also fit God as Lord or King. The list is illustrative of the praiseworthy attributes of God, that is, the character of God that moves us to praise. A typical example follows:

> "Sing praises to God, sing praises; sing praises to our King, sing praises. For God is the King of all the earth; sing to him a psalm of praise. God reigns over the nations; God is seated on his holy throne."   (Ps 47:6,7)

---

[3] The word praise is cited 168 times in the Psalms.

Some Praiseworthy Attributes of God

God/ Lord	Ex 15:2; Ps 9:1; 42:11; 68:4
Worthiness	2 Sam 22:4; Rev 5:12
Holiness	2 Chron 20:21; Ps 22:3; 97:12; 103:1
Awesome	Ps 68:35; 99:3
Righteousness/ Justice	Ps 7:17; 101:1; Dan 4:37
Living	Ps 18:46
King	Ps 47:6,7
Gloriousness/ Splendour	Neh 9:5; Ps 66:2; 71:8; 72:19; 148:13
Greatness/ Majesty	Deut 32:3; Ps 99:3; 104:1; 145:3; 150:2
Wisdom	Dan 2:20
Creator	2 Chron 2:12
Power	Dan 2:20
Goodness/ Kindness	Ps 54:6; 106:1
Love/ Faithfulness	Ps 59:17; 71:22; 89:5; 106:1; 117:2; 138:2; Is 25:1; 63:7
Compassion/ Counsel/ Comfort	Ps 16:7; 2 Cor 1:3
Saviour/ Redeemer	Ps 42:11; 71:23; Luke 1:68
Rock/ Strength/ Fortress	2 Sam 22:47; Ps 59:17; 144:1
Joy and delight	Ps 43:4
Salvation/ Rescue	Ex 15:2; 18:10; Jer 20:13

God's Actions

It is of course not only God's character but also His deeds that spark people's praise. The two are closely related since God's deeds are His character in action. Thus we praise Him as Creator and more specifically for His creative acts. We praise Him as Saviour and Redeemer and especially for saving or rescuing us or others. Indeed, it is the very experience of God's actions that lead us to understand his nature and character. For example, the willing and sacrificial gift of His Son reveals to us God's face of love[4].

The Old Testament is one story in many instalments of God's saving acts among His people. At times, when the people are fully aware of what God has done on their behalf, they burst into unrestrained praise. One example of this is when God rescues them from the might of Pharaoh's army at the Red Sea[5]. Moses and the Israelites, Miriam and the women, praise God with exuberant song and dance, marvelling in God's greatness, majesty, power, holiness and the unfailing love of God that is evident in the miraculous intervention. The people sing:

> "Who among the gods is like you, O Lord? Who is like you – majestic in holiness, awesome in glory, working wonders?"   (Ex 15:11)

A rather different example, and this time the praises are on the lips of a pagan king, arises through the faithfulness of Daniel's companions[6]. The Babylonian king, Nebuchadnezzar, had recently constructed a ninety foot golden image and commanded all his citizens to worship. Shadrach, Meshach and Abednego defy the king's command and are thrown into the fiery furnace. They are miraculously delivered by divine intervention and this prompts the king to praise God:

> "Praise be to the God of Shadrach, Meshach and Abednego, who has sent his angel and rescued his servants!"   (Dan 4:28)

Of course, divine intervention is not limited to the Old Testament. On numerous occasions Jesus' miraculous healings or the Holy Spirit's divine intervention prompt the people to praise God. For example,

---

[4] John 3:16; Rom 5:8

[5] Ex 15:1-21

[6] The story is recounted in Dan ch 3

Jesus' healing of the paralytic, brought by the four friends, causes both patient and onlookers to praise God:

> "Immediately he (the paralytic) stood up in front of them, took what he had been lying on and went home praising God. Everyone was amazed and gave praise to God. They were filled with awe and said, "We have seen remarkable things today." (Luke 5:25,26)

Likewise, we see the response of praise when Peter heals the cripple at the temple gate. Luke records that immediately the man:

> "Jumped to his feet and began to walk. Then he went with them into the temple courts, walking and jumping and praising God." (Acts 3:8)

In a rather different example Peter is led to preach in the home of Cornelius where all his friends, neighbours and relatives are gathered. Disconcertingly, in the middle of the message, the Holy Spirit came upon the people with power. And Peter, to his astonishment, hears the gathered assembly 'speaking in tongues and praising God'.[7]

All these, and many other biblical examples, demonstrate clearly that God at work in our lives and the lives of others is a focus for praise.

The Manner and Means of Praise

Not only does the Bible describe what motivated people to praise but also how they praised God – both the attitudes of heart and mind that accompanied praise and also the ways in which they praised God. One thing that needs to be clearly understood is that praise is not a personal matter between us and God. Nearly always in the Bible, praise is a public declaration or proclamation of who God is and what He has done. Thus we are called to:

> "Sing to the Lord, praise his name; proclaim his salvation day after day.
> Declare his glory among the nations, his marvellous deeds among all peoples." (Ps 96:2,3)

This is not a private conversation with God but a public announcement of the greatness and wonderful acts of God. In like manner Peter reminds believers that they are called to declare God's praises[8].

---

[7] Acts 10:44-46

[8] 1 Pet 2:9

Attitude of praise

Although every individual has a different experience of God and different reasons for praise, yet there appear to be several constants in the attitudes of people who praise God. The dominant emotion that accompanies praise is one of joy and gladness. For example, at the rededication of the temple under King Hezekiah we read that the Levites: 'sang praises with gladness'[9]. Almost invariably psalms of praise reveal a note of joy in the heart of the worshipper. Thus the psalmist worships with the words:

> "I will praise you, O Lord, with all my heart; I will tell of all your wonders. I will be glad and rejoice in you; I will sing praise to your name, O Most High." (Ps 9:1,2)

and again:

> "My lips will shout for joy when I sing praise to you – I, whom you have redeemed." (Ps 71:23)

Elsewhere the psalmist encourages the worshipper to:

> "Sing joyfully to the Lord, you righteous." (Ps 33:1)

and:

> "Shout for joy to the Lord, all the earth. Worship the Lord with gladness; come before him with joyful songs."   (Ps 100:1,2)

If we are really aware of who God is and what He has done for us, inevitably we will praise Him joyfully. But note, as worship leaders we cannot prescribe joy or force worshippers to be joyful. Joy should be spontaneous and natural. Like the psalmist,[10] we need to open the people's eyes to see who God is, what he has done and is doing in our lives today – then people will truly praise joyfully. As the Scriptures declare: 'In His presence is fullness of joy'[11]. Our role is to lead God's people into His presence where their joy will be complete and overflowing.

---

[9] 2 Chr 29:30

[10] Psalm 100 is an excellent example of this. The Psalmist encourages the people to praise God joyfully and then motivates by giving the reasons why we should do so. He doesn't assume that the people are automatically joyful but rather he focuses the people's attention on God's character and deeds which are reasons for joy,

[11] Ps 16:10 (AV)

Praise

The second predominant attitude is that our praise should be wholehearted – coming from the very depths of our being and encompassing all that we are. The passage quoted above from Psalm 9 contains this idea as the psalmist declares: 'I will praise you, O Lord, with all my heart...'. The same thought is expressed rather differently in Psalm 103 verse 1:

"Praise the Lord, O my soul; all my inmost being, praise his holy name."

But the meaning is the same. The whole of our being, heart, mind and soul is called into relationship with God in praise. This means that as we praise: we think about God and His character – we know his goodness towards us; we get emotional about God and His doings – we feel his love for us and long to reciprocate; we open our spirits to the Spirit's touch – so that we can praise God in ways beyond words; we open our lips to declare, and our bodies to act out, the praises of the one who so wonderfully made us, saved us and called us to be His own.

Means of Praise

When we understand that praise is a joyful, public proclamation of the greatness of God from the depths of our being, then it follows that the means of praising God must be appropriate. Praise necessarily must be seen and heard so that others, both believer and unbeliever alike, hear and understand. Praise will often be excited, exuberant and sometimes loud – consonant with the amazing message that we proclaim. Let's look together briefly at some of the ways that the people praised God in Bible times.

Firstly, they used their voices to call out and shout God's praises. Thus God's people shouted in praise at the laying of the foundations of the new Temple[12]; the Psalmist personally 'cried out' to God in praise[13] and elsewhere encouraged the people to 'shout for joy' to the Lord[14] as an act of praise. The Psalmist puts it like this:

"Praise our God, O peoples, let the sound of his praise be heard ..."[15]

---

[12] Ezra 3:11

[13] Ps 66:17; 71:23

[14] Ps 98:4, 100:1

[15] Ps 66:6

Our God is worth celebrating and we want other people to hear too! But of course praise is not primarily about being noisy; it is about proclaiming. Thus King David writes that as he worships so he is:

"... proclaiming aloud your praise and telling of all your wonderful deeds." (Ps 26:7)

In some ways, like King David, personal praise can be a form of public testimony as to the goodness of God. Sometimes words of praise were said, recited, prayed or shouted out in unison or responsively[16].

Secondly, and this involves by far the majority of references, God's praises are sung[17]. This does not automatically involve musical accompaniment. Sometimes, especially at major celebrations in the Temple, musical instruments would have been used and are mentioned in the biblical text. On other occasions, especially in the home or on informal occasions, the people would have sung without accompaniment. This is almost certainly the case when Jesus sang one of the psalms with the disciples at the Passover meal[18] and when Paul and Silas sang hymns in prison at midnight[19].

Thirdly, the people praised God with music. Sometimes this was an accompaniment of the singing, sometimes as part of a procession of praise, sometimes with dancing, or sometimes simply as a musical expression of praise[20]. Perhaps Psalm 150 is the passage that most dramatically focuses the role of musical instruments in praise. The psalm opens with a reminder that praise is to be directed to God for His acts of power and His surpassing greatness and then emphasises the role of a whole range[21] of musical instruments used to praise God.

---

[16] Neh 12:24

[17] A selection of references to sung praises are given as follows: 1 Chron 16:9; 2 Chron 5:13; 29:30; Ps 18:49; 21:13; 30:4; 40:3; 57:9; 66:2; 68:32; 71:22; 96:2; 101:1; 105:2; 135:3; 146:2; Rom 15:,9,11.

[18] Mat 26:30

[19] Acts 16:25

[20] 1 Chron 23:5

[21] This, of course, should not be considered as an exhaustive list, although it covers a wide range of wind, string and percussion instruments.

Praise

Interestingly, praise is not limited to the use of our voices, song and music. Praise is associated with: giving of freewill offerings[22], fulfilling of vows[23], writing for future generations[24], studying and learning God's Word[25] and fellowship and unity with fellow believers[26].

Because of its exuberant and demonstrative nature bodily movements frequently accompany praise. People praise God in procession to the temple[27], with dancing[28], in standing[29], in raising hands[30] and in bowing down and prostrating oneself before the Lord[31]. Interestingly it is difficult to find a firm biblical basis for the 'clap offering' that is so prominent in some circles.[32] However, it is quite clear that our bodies as well as our lips are to be used is declaring the glory of God.

It is evident from this brief study that praising God involves far more than simply singing His praises. These other ways of praising need to become part of our corporate worship so that we can praise with the whole of our being.

---

[22] Lev 19:24; Ps 54:6
[23] Ps 61:8; 65:1
[24] Ps 102:18
[25] Ps 119; 7, 12, 108, 171
[26] Rom 15:7
[27] Ps 100:4
[28] Ps 149:3; 150:4
[29] 1 Chron 23:30; Neh 9:5;
[30] Ps 63:4; 134:2
[31] 1 Chron 29:20; Ps 66:4
[32] There are no specific references to a 'clap offering' in the Old Testament. Clapping hands in the Old Testament has a variety of meanings including: recognition of kingship (2 Kings 11:12); acknowledgement of God's sovereignty by the nations (Ps 47:1,2); anger (Num 24:10); scorn and derision (Job 34:37); rejoicing at the downfall of evil doers (Nahum 3:19); the metaphorical description of the praise offered by the natural realm. (Is 55:12 and Ps 98:8). There does not appear to be any formal 'clap offering' associated with the regular Israelite worship.

Other Aspects of Praise

Although we have discussed the reasons for praise and the ways in which people praise in the Bible, there still remain one or two other important aspects of praise that require mention. These include the people and place of praise, the relationship of praise and thanksgiving and the power or effect of praise.

The People of Praise

The Bible is clear that the whole of the created realm in heaven and on earth is called to acknowledge God the Creator through bringing the praise that is due His Name. In the psalms this is seen to include: the individual worshipper[33], God's people[34], the saints and the upright[35], the council of elders[36], the congregation, the great assembly and crowds[37], the servants of the Lord[38], all the nations, kingdoms and peoples[39], children[40], the poor and needy[41], kings of the earth[42] and everything that has breath[43]. But even this list is not exhaustive; praise extends beyond people to include both the natural and heavenly realms. Thus praise is expected from: the sun, moon and stars[44]; the heaven, earth and seas[45]; the heavens, angels and the heavenly hosts[46] and all that God has made[47].

---

[33] Ps 103:1
[34] Ps 79:13
[35] Ps 30:4; 33:1; 52:9; 64:10
[36] Ps 107:32
[37] Ps 22:22; 35:18; 68:26; 109:30
[38] Ps 135:3
[39] Ps 18:48; 57:9; 67:3,5; 68:32; 117:1
[40] Ps 8:2
[41] Ps 74:21
[42] Ps 138:4
[43] Ps 150:6
[44] Ps 148:3
[45] Ps 69:34
[46] Ps 89:5; 103:20,21
[47] Ps 103:22; 145:10

Praise

The whole of creation and all the peoples of the world are called into a timeless act of praise to our King that extends: 'day after day'[48], 'through the watches of the night'[49], 'as long as I live'[50], 'from generation to generation'[51] and from 'everlasting to everlasting'[52]. God's praise is to be heard in the sanctuary[53], in the home[54], and to the ends of the earth[55].

The heart of the Gospel of Jesus Christ is realising the vision of the Psalmist in bringing all peoples, in every place and in all times to know, acknowledge and praise their Creator.

Praise and Thanksgiving

We mentioned earlier that praise is distinct from thanksgiving but the two are intimately connected in that thanksgiving may well up into praise and praise may spill over into thanksgiving. As we thank God for specific blessings and gifts, so almost inevitably our worship goes beyond giving thanks for the gift, to praise for the giver. King David's beautiful prayer at the thanksgiving gift day perfectly illustrates this close connection:

> "David praised the LORD in the presence of the whole assembly, saying, "Praise be to you, O LORD, God of our father Israel, from everlasting to everlasting. Yours, O LORD, is the greatness and the power and the glory and the majesty and the splendor, for everything in heaven and earth is yours. Yours, O LORD, is the kingdom; you are exalted as head over all. Wealth and honor come from you; you are the ruler of all things. In your hands are strength and power to exalt and give strength to all. Now, our God, *we give you thanks, and praise* your glorious name." (1 Chr 29:10-13)

Several other examples may be found in the biblical texts[56].

---

[48] Ps 96:2
[49] Ps 63:6
[50] Ps 104:33
[51] Ps 79:13
[52] 1 Chron 16:36
[53] Ps 116:19
[54] Ps 63:6
[55] Ps 48:10
[56] See for example: Ps 7:17; 35:18; 69:30; 100:4; 106:1

The Power of Praise

Does anything happen when we praise? The answer of the Scriptures and many Christian testimonies is a resounding yes! Somehow as we praise God it opens the channels for God's blessing in our lives. Praise, or more broadly worship, is transformational because it changes our focus from our personal circumstances to God. It liberates us from being overwhelmed and crushed by what is happening around us and opens us to God's glory that transforms the humble stable or the dark prison cell.

Paul and Silas, while faithfully preaching the Gospel, had been arrested, stripped, severely beaten, thrown into prison and chained in their prison cell. Not happy circumstances! Their reaction – they pray out loud and sing hymns of praise[57]. They declare and proclaim the glory of God, and their fellow prisoners listen. As they praise so God works miraculously and the result is that the jailer and his family are saved and the other prisoners must surely have been touched by God's power at work. Here we can see how praise opened the way for God to act in a dramatic way.

In the Old Testament, praise was often associated with warfare. Israel's most notable victories occurred not through their own skills in battle but by the intervention of the King of kings. On one such occasion the combined hordes came against King Jehoshaphat and the people of Judah. But the king puts his trust in God and the biblical text records:

> "After consulting the people, Jehoshaphat appointed men to sing to the LORD and to praise him for the splendor of his holiness as they went out at the head of the army, saying: "Give thanks to the LORD, for his love endures forever." *As they began to sing and praise, the LORD set ambushes* against the men of Ammon and Moab and Mount Seir who were invading Judah, and they were defeated." (2 Chron 20:21,22)

Now as Christians we are no longer involved in physical warfare but we certainly need God's help in the spiritual battle and praise is one aspect of that struggle[58].

---

[57] Acts 16:25

[58] See Eph 6:10-18 for Paul's description of the Christian armour.

This is also the Psalmist's personal testimony[59]. He describes his personal circumstances graphically as: 'a slimy pit', and 'mud and mire'. But God intervenes, giving him 'a new song ... a hymn of praise' and rescues him from his distress. Through God's intervention and the Psalmist's praise of God '... many will see and fear and put their trust in the Lord.' Thus praise in difficult circumstances or in recognition of God's rescue is an effective channel of witness.

Just like prayer, of which it is a part, praise changes things.

Practical Praise in Corporate Worship

We have looked in some detail at praise in the Bible; now we need to see how the biblical practice of praise is relevant to our corporate worship. In a later chapter we shall see how praise can be integrated into the worship service or liturgy, but at this point we simply want to affirm the importance of praise and look at some practical forms of expression.

Context and Culture

In interpreting the Bible and applying it to our own situation we must realise that God's Word is always expressed in a culturally related way. Thus, whereas biblical principles remain unchanged, practices need to be interpreted for our times. For example, Jesus instructed His disciples: 'If someone forces you to go one mile, go with him two miles.'[60] This referred to the obligation of local citizens to carry the goods and belongings of Roman soldiers a distance of up to one mile. Clearly we are no longer under that obligation and so the principle of 'the second mile' has to be given new meaning in our current day.

Furthermore, Old Testament practice must be seen and understood in the light of the New. For example, the sacrificial worship system was an integral part of the Old Testament revelation but it is not continued in the New nor practised by the Church today[61]. The reason is that

---

[59] Ps 40:1-3

[60] Mat 5:41

[61] Hence the Church does not require *priests* to lead worship.

Christ's death on the cross represents the final sacrifice for sin, rendering any further animal sacrifice unnecessary[62]. Thus in the New Testament, sacrifice as a continuing principle of worship is reinterpreted in terms of lives wholly surrendered to God[63] and the sacrifice of praise and good works[64].

Musical Instruments

A particular example of the above discussion is the use of musical instruments in worship. We have seen that the Old Testament strongly endorses the use of music and musical instruments as part of worship. The biblical principle would seem to be that music should be a legitimate part of contemporary worship[65]. However, it would be wrong to take literally the contents of Psalm 150 and prescribe that Christians should only use trumpets, harps, lyres, tambourines *etc*. The list is clearly exemplary and written in the context of the instruments available at the time[66].

Worship in Action

Body language refers to the messages that are conveyed by our facial expressions and our bodies. A trained listener or counsellor will often focus on the body language in addition to words in order to 'hear' what

---

[62] Heb 10:8-10

[63] Rom 12:1

[64] Heb 13:15,16

[65] There are some Christians who would refute this and only allow the unaccompanied voice in worship. Their argument is the *silence* of the New Testament. Thus, whereas Jesus and the early Christians undoubtedly sang there is no evidence of musical instruments. However, it is unsafe to argue against musical accompaniment from the *silence* of the New Testament since music is so clearly advocated in the Old Testament. At very least, if music were to be abolished one would expect some recorded teaching from Jesus or the apostles to that effect. It may well be that musical instruments were not relevant to the early missionary times when Christians needed to be mobile, met in homes, had limited resources and had to conduct worship in secret (and hence quietly) for fear of arrest and imprisonment.

[66] In the same light it is rather mistaken to suppose that ram's horns of the type used in the Old Testament, and specially imported from Israel at great expense, add a spiritual dimension or render the worship more biblical.

Praise

someone is saying. However, we should also remember that body language is to some extent culturally conditioned. This means that, whereas the Bible endorses the expression of praise with our bodies, we need to think carefully how far such expression is appropriate and helpful in our own church, set in its own cultural context.

Of course, it may also be that there are contemporary cultural expressions unknown in biblical times that can helpfully be introduced into our worship. One of these *may* be clapping. As mentioned earlier, there is no clear biblical precedent for the use of clapping in worship, but it is widely used in contemporary society to show appreciation or adulation whether at a theatre show, a pop concert or a political rally. Some might wish to go further and import whistles, banners and football rattles, or project video clips or even discharge fireworks as part of the celebration.

But one must be careful. Borrowing from secular society can be syncretistic[67] and this was the reason why many Christian missionaries rejected the inclusion of pagan music and symbols in Christian worship. We must never simply use the secular because it is attractive, but rather think how far can it legitimately be used in God's praise, how far can it be transformed to become a genuine expression of our Christian worship?

Praise in Practice

It was pointed out at the beginning of this chapter that very often the way we express praise is very limited. In this section we are going to examine how we can begin to develop our praise in corporate worship, making use of biblical practices. Of course in reality, what aspects we use in leading our own corporate worship will depend on the worship experience of the worshippers, the facilities, skills and the readiness of the people to try new things. So we start where we are, we use what we

---

[67] Allowing the absorption of differing aspects or practices into the Christian faith that are unbiblical or contradict the Gospel. For example, the use of amulets or lucky charms by Christians as a means of protection undermines a total dependence upon God and opens the believer to attack by demonic forces. A rather different aspect is multi-faith worship where the use of elements from other religious traditions legitimises the truth of those faiths and undermines the uniqueness of the Christian message.

have got and slowly begin to build new ways of praise, and new ways of worship.

Song

The songs we choose, the musical accompaniment, the people who sing and our actions can help us vary how we praise God in song. The starting point is the choice of song. Choose songs that are not only suitable musically but have good words, in particular, that feed our minds and provide us with the reason and motivation for praising God. Praise songs should mainly focus on who God is and what he has done and is doing in our lives. Don't just use choruses but incorporate hymns that tell a story and develop a particular theme or biblical truth.

If it is appropriate to use short praise choruses repetitively, then provide variety. Some might be sung in parts, sometimes men or women only, sometimes unaccompanied. Try and vary posture. Don't expect the congregation to stand for 40 minutes with their arms raised. Help the congregation to speak with their bodies. If the lyrics are exalting Christ, lifting up His Name, raising Him higher then our raised arms can express that. If we are bowing before him in song, then it might be appropriate to kneel[68].

Sometimes it may be right to use a solo singer, or a choir item to focus the praise. But remember, this is not a concert performance; the singer need not be at the front; she or he can sing from the centre or the back of the congregation. Applause is usually inappropriate as it is almost inevitably focussed on the singer rather than God.

Music

Whereas congregations can sing beautifully without musical accompaniment, music does add another dimension to praise. But it is vital that the musicians are sensitive to the worship and play appropriately. Unfortunately some players automatically assume that praise means being loud! The reality is that there needs to be variety and contrast. Volume needs to be appropriate to the theme being expressed and needs to be varied. Similarly, there often could be a

---

[68] What is possible will to some extent depend on the furnishings and the space available in the worship centre.

Praise

greater variety in the range of instruments used – wind instruments in particular, such as the trumpet, saxophone and flute, add a very distinctive contribution.

Music need not always be professional. In worship, especially where children are present, simple rhythm instruments[69] can be used throughout the body of the congregation to add another dimension to the praise.

Movement

Without doubt heartfelt expressive praise requires movement. Sometimes this will be orchestrated, sometimes spontaneous. It is probably better for the congregation to follow the example of the leader or leaders[70] than be dragooned into action[71]. The important thing is that the action should be from the heart and expressive of the aspect of praise.

On special occasions a procession of praise into, or around, the worship centre, whilst singing, may be very meaningful. As we praise, to raise hands to exalt the name of Jesus or to kneel or fall down before God's throne can enable us to speak to God without words. Many of us will feel like dancing in exuberance at God's goodness and move to the music or clap our hands. Sometimes we may use a more formal liturgical or culturally related dance to praise God.

Acclamations

Our praise can be punctuated with acclamations. These need not be part of a formal liturgy but can be easily learnt by a congregation. The Bible is full of them. Some useable examples are given below:

    Leader: For great is the Lord!

    People: And most worthy of praise![72]

---

[69] Instruments such as rice shakers or rhythm sticks can be easily made very cheaply.

[70] Not only the worship leader but the spiritual leaders within the church can encourage the congregation by their example.

[71] The feeling of joy and its expression comes as we are drawn into the presence of God – it cannot be commanded.

[72] 1 Chron 16:25; Ps 48:1; Ps 96:4

Leader: Give thanks to the Lord!
People: His love endures for ever![73]

Leader: O Lord, open my lips!
People: And my mouth will declare your praise![74]

Leader: He is Lord ! (King)
People: He is Lord of lords! (King of kings)[75]

Leader: Hallelujah!
People: For the Lord our God the Almighty Reigns![76]

These responses are short, easily memorised and can be introduced at different parts of the service as appropriate. One can also use a series of responses in succession. They are more easily spoken when standing.

Scripture Readings

Acclamations are helpful in introducing pithy Bible sayings, but we also need to have greater exposure to the Scriptures in order to praise God. Quite apart from any lectionary reading, or Bible passage chosen to illustrate the theme of the sermon, we can use short Bible readings to lead the congregation in praising God. These can either be read expressively by an individual or perhaps responsively by the congregation[77]. The psalms are rich in suitable passages, but any texts that focus on the attributes of God or his actions would be suitable.

Prayer

Praise of course is not limited to song. The service should include prayers of praise whether led by the leader or articulated by the congregation. (See the previous chapter on Prayer for various ideas).

---

[73] 2 Chron 5:13

[74] Ps 51:15

[75] Rev 17:14

[76] Rev 19:6

[77] But only do responsive readings if nearly all the congregation have the same Bible version or the words can be displayed on a screen or in the bulletin, otherwise the result will be chaotic.

Praise

The content of the prayer should focus on the attributes or actions of God. Some very moving biblical prayers can be used or adapted for corporate worship. Part of King David's prayer at the thanksgiving gift day is given below[78]:

> "Praise be to you, O LORD, God of our father Israel, from everlasting to everlasting. Yours, O LORD, is the greatness and the power and the glory and the majesty and the splendor, for everything in heaven and earth is yours. Yours, O LORD, is the kingdom; you are exalted as head over all. Wealth and honor come from you; you are the ruler of all things. In your hands are strength and power to exalt and give strength to all. Now, our God, we give you thanks, and praise your glorious name."

Testimony

It may perhaps seem odd to include testimony within a section on praise, but testimony should inspire praise. Testimony is not about someone's life story or what they have achieved for God, but rather what God has done for them or through them. Testimony can be used within a time of praise for people to relate what God is doing. The response to the testimony should be a prayer of praise and thanksgiving to God for all that he has done.

Offering

Finally we may wish to use our time of offering as an opportunity for praise. We can praise God in a practical way not just with our words but also in giving our gifts and tithes to God. Instead of just passing around the bag or offering plate we intentionally make this a part of our praise. The offering can be introduced with a comment such as:

> "Now let us praise God through the giving of our tithes and offerings. As we give to God let us do so joyfully and willingly so that His name will be praised and glorified. As we give, we will sing hymn …"

On a special occasion such as an anniversary gift day the giving could be conducted in a procession of praise and thanksgiving with the whole congregation moving to the front in turn to offer their gifts to the Lord.

---

[78] 1Chron 29:10-13

Summary

In this chapter we have discovered the centrality of praise in the Bible as part of worship. We have seen that praise is concerned with proclaiming the attributes of God and His wondrous deeds. We have begun to recognise that praise is more than singing and have considered various other practical ways to encourage the congregation to praise God from the depth of their being.

7 – Participation

The opening chapters of this book introduced us to three important principles, specifically that worship involves: the whole of life, the whole person and the whole congregation. We have already begun to see how these principles are applied in worship, but in this chapter we will bring them under closer scrutiny. In particular, we shall think about how our daily lives and activities can be integrated into our worship, and how we can fully participate as individuals and as a body in corporate worship. In other words, we will see how worship can touch and be touched by our lives; how we can contribute individually to worship and how we can worship together with our brothers and sisters in Christ.

The People of God

But before we begin to look in detail at participatory worship we need to think briefly about who we are as we come together to worship with others. The New Testament uses several different words to describe our status before God and our relationship with other believers. Some of those particularly relevant to corporate worship will be discussed below.

New Testament Terms

Interestingly the New Testament writers rarely use the word 'Christian' to describe believers[1]. More common descriptions include 'disciples', 'the people of God', and 'saints'[2]. However, there are three further descriptions or metaphors that are particularly helpful in thinking about corporate worship and we will consider them in turn.

---

[1] The first mention comes in the church at Antioch (Acts 11:26). Other references are: Acts 26:28 and 1 Pet 4:16

[2] The term saints is frequently used in Pauline letters to refer to believers - see Rom 1:7 and 2 Cor 1:1. This term reminds us of the Christian calling to be a holy people

Church

The word church[3], as used in Bible translations such as the *New International Version,* translates the Greek word *ekklesia* that refers to a group of people who are 'called out', to gather together for a common purpose. In the Old Testament[4], *ekklesia* referred to the Israelites who were called out of slavery in Egypt to be God's people with the common purpose of serving Him.

In the New Testament the word is used in two distinct ways. Firstly, in a secular context, it is used to describe the trade union meeting of silversmiths in Ephesus[5]. The workers were called out from their homes or businesses to meet together for the common purpose of deciding what to do about the Christians who were ruining their trade in silver idols.

Secondly, the word is used to describe the gathering together of Christians[6]. When *ekklesia* is applied to Christians it *always* refers to the people of God who are called out of the world to meet together for the common purpose of worship. Thus in the Bible the word church refers to people and *never* a structure or a building. As the Church we are God's people who are called together to worship Him. This reminds us that, whereas buildings are helpful for worship, yet the people are always of paramount importance.

Body of Christ

One of the most important metaphors used in the New Testament to describe our status as Christians is the 'Body of Christ'[7]. This is a vital

---

[3] We use the word 'church' to refer to the local community of Christians and 'Church' to the whole company of believers throughout the world. Because the word church has a variety of meanings in contemporary English (people/ building/ institution *etc*) a more precise and helpful translation of *ekklesia* is congregation.

[4] Strictly the term only appears in the *Septuagint,* the Greek translation of the Hebrew original.

[5] The word *ekklesia* is here translated as 'assembly' (Acts 19:32,41)

[6] See for example: Rom 16:1, 4, 5; 1 Cor 1:2

[7] This meaning of this metaphor is detailed in three separate Pauline letters: Romans 12:4-8; 1 Cor 12:12-31; Eph 4:1-16.

picture as it not only shows our relationship with Christ as the 'head' of the body but also our relationship with other members of the body. As a church there are many members but we are *one* because we are one body. Each member has particular gifts and skills to be used for the benefit of the body. Furthermore, we are all interdependent – what affects one member affects us all.

This image is particularly of value when we think about the meaning of corporate worship. The word corporate is derived from the Latin word *corpus* meaning 'body' and so literally we are talking about body (of Christ) worship. This means that our worship involves the whole body working together to honour and glorify God. The worship uses individual skills and abilities but embraces and includes every member. Furthermore, something special occurs when we meet together as a body that is distinct from our individual worship of God[8].

Royal Priesthood

The third image that speaks powerfully about corporate worship is 'Royal Priesthood'. Peter, writing to Christian believers, states:

> "But you are a chosen people, a royal priesthood, a holy nation, a people belonging to God, that you may declare the praises of him who called you out of darkness into his wonderful light." (1 Pet 2:9)

In the New Testament the words translated as priest(s) or priesthood are used in one of four distinct ways. Firstly, to refer to the Jewish priests or Chief Priests who served in the Jerusalem temple[9]. Secondly, to refer to pagan priests such as the priest of Zeus[10]. Thirdly, in the book of Hebrews, Jesus is repeatedly described as our great High Priest[11]. Lastly, the term priests or priesthood is applied to Christian believers[12].

---

[8] Note the promise of Jesus in Mat 18:20.

[9] For example, Zechariah, John the Baptist's father (Luke 1:5), or Caiaphas the High Priest (Mat 26:3,57)

[10] Acts 14:13

[11] See for example Heb 4:14,15; 5:6; 6:20; 7:26; 8:1

[12] 1 Pet 2:5,9; Rev 1:6; 5:10; 20:6. But note there is no reference to an individual serving as a Christian priest. Thus, when Paul cites Christ's gifts or provision for the church he refers to: apostles, prophets, evangelists, pastors and teachers (Eph 4:11) but not once to priests.

In the New Testament believers are *corporately* referred to as priests or a priesthood on no less than five occasions. However, the letter to the Hebrews makes it clear that Christ *alone* is our priest – the intermediate between man and God – this is why, for example, we end our prayers 'In the name of Jesus'. It follows then that the worship leader does not have a priestly role; rather she or he leads the Royal Priesthood in offering their praises to God.

Peter elaborates this idea when he writes:

> "As you come to him, the living Stone—rejected by men but chosen by God and precious to him— you also, like living stones, are being built into a spiritual house to be a holy priesthood, offering spiritual sacrifices acceptable to God through Jesus Christ." (1 Pet 2:4,5)

Not only are we to be a holy priesthood but also, as we come to Jesus in our lives and in our worship, we are being changed and transformed to become together a spiritual house or temple for our God. In this light we need to put far more emphasis on a consecrated (holy) people than a consecrated building as a prerequisite to worship God.

Summary

All three images detailed above emphasise the importance of the people in corporate worship. The Church is God's people, called out of darkness to unite as one Body in order, as a Royal Priesthood, to declare His praises. It is the people's worship. The role of the worship leader or worship team is to facilitate that worship.

Participatory Worship

Touching Daily Lives

For worship to be corporate it must be relevant and touch people's lives. This involves various aspects such as: language, culture, and memories or past experiences. It must connect with our lives, specifically our families, church, community, workplace and the wider world. It will also include our inner feelings and experiences such as our hopes and fears, struggles and victory, success and failure, weaknesses and empowerment, sickness and health, poverty and riches, life and death. Clearly as worship leader or preacher we need to know our people and their condition and allow the worship to speak to these needs in a language the people can understand.

Language and Culture

One of the priorities of Bible societies around the world is to translate the Bible into people's mother tongues. This is a mammoth task because of the huge number of distinct language groups – even here in Sabah there are over 30 tribal languages. One might suppose it would be less effort to teach the people a new language rather than to translate the Scriptures into a little known or little used language. However, this overlooks the importance of using one's own mother tongue. The language that we learn as a child in the home has a very special place in our heart and life and can speak to us in a way that no second, or foreign, language can do.

The same is true of the language of worship and preaching – it needs to be the language that is owned by the worshippers. This is of course problematic even in a monolingual community since different age groups may have different vocabularies. An elderly person in Britain may be more at home in the language of the King James Bible for worship whereas this may be hard work for younger adults and meaningless to a teenager. Each group, even children, has its own specialised vocabulary and culture.

It is vital for participatory worship to try to use a language and vocabulary that is generally understood. The hymns and prayers should be in an idiom that enables the people to worship. In mixed age worship it is better to have ingredients that can be understood by all, although there may be room for one or two items particularly chosen for the minority groups such as the very young or the elderly.

Intercessory Prayer

In our earlier chapter on prayer we discussed in detail various ways of praying but said very little about the content of intercessory prayer. Intercessory prayer needs to have a balanced content and one way is to pray in an ever-expanding spiral starting with personal needs. For example, a helpful progression could be: self/ family/ church/ community/ nation/ world. Using this pattern we can pray in a way that touches peoples lives; for example, each section can be expanded as follows:

- Self – personal needs (spiritual growth/ unemployment/ sickness/ important decisions/ grief)
- Family – family needs (faith in Christ/ health/ education)
- Church – local and national (pastor & leaders/ unity/ growth in maturity/ witness/ special projects)
- Community – needs within local community (outreach and evangelism/ specific social needs or individuals)
- Nation – National leaders (Government/ Justice/ Christian principles and ethics)
- The World – World needs (Leaders/ Mission/ Social needs)

If we know the congregation and their needs, and are alert to what is happening in the news, then we can lead prayers in a way that touches their lives. It is probably always worth glancing at a newspaper, or tuning into the news, or checking the internet just before leaving for the church service so that you can be up to date with prayer needs.

In the event that an individual or a church family is facing a particular crisis or need, the church as the body of Christ can pray for them. Prayer should always be sensitive; sometimes it may be appropriate to ask permission to pray for people by name. The local church should always be praying for those who are sick or bereaved or facing some particular difficulty. Some churches use an intercessions book that is made available before the service for members to write down specific prayer needs.[13] These are then addressed during the prayer time.

The church can also participate in people's lives when they are facing particular challenge or special ministry responsibility. It is good, for example, to pray for: young people facing examinations; students leaving home (and church) to study or work in another town; the

---

[13] For example, the book may be placed on a table in the foyer or entrance of the meeting place.

Participation 113

Sunday school teachers; the newly appointed Church Council members and so on. Sometimes it is good too to pray specifically for the pastor and church leaders. The church should also be praying regularly for people sent out from the church to a wider ministry either at home or overseas. In this way the church continues to participate in their lives.

Through targeted intercessory prayer the people are enabled to integrate their lives more fully into the worship.

Testimony

We have already touched briefly on testimony in the previous chapter on praise. However, it is important to mention it in this chapter on participation as testimony allows individuals to contribute to the worship as well as to bring their lives into the corporate worship in a special way. Testimony is very important as it inspires praise and thanksgiving, illustrates the power of prayer and shows how God works in people's lives both as a warning and an example.

This need not of course be limited to speaking about a conversion experience but includes relating how the Lord is continuing to work in our life[14]. This can be particularly helpful in worship as the congregation begin to understand that we worship a living Lord who is active in the lives of His people today. Some churches have a regular slot for testimony within the worship service, whereas others introduce it from time to time, as seems appropriate. It would, for example, be relevant to have one or two members share about how they became Christians at an evangelistic service. Similarly, it is most helpful for baptism candidates to share how they came to faith in Christ as their Saviour and Lord.

Unfortunately, the opportunity for sharing testimony can be abused. For example, it may be the same people who speak every week and the testimony may be too focussed on themselves rather than God. There

---

[14] In the sixties a bishop who was serving in Africa shared with us his experience. He was describing to an African congregation how God had been working in his life when he was interrupted by a loud voice from the back of the church with the challenge: 'Bishop! That's old news – what is God doing in your life today?' This is a reminder that we need to experience God's ongoing work in our life.

probably need to be some ground-rules for testimony such as, the testimony should:
- Be short – perhaps 5 minutes maximum.
- Bring glory to God – not unduly focus on the person.
- Be recent or relevant – not repeating something that happened a long time ago.
- Be first hand – not telling someone else's story.

A helpful arrangement is for those who want to testify, to talk with the leader before the service for a preliminary screening as to suitability. Alternatively, the testimony might be suggested or recommended by the leader of a small group or cell group who knows something of what God has been doing in the members' lives.

It may be necessary to open the eyes of the congregation as to the things that are appropriate to share. These will include not only positive aspects such as: a friend's conversion after years of prayer; or personal healing through prayer ministry; but also the presence of God through failure and suffering, or the conviction of sin.

I shall never forget the service where a church member testified that the Lord had convicted her to return her driving licence to the authorities. The reason? Her driving-school fee had included a bribe for the examiner! This was shared with humility and provided a powerful lesson for Asian Christians constantly confronted by the problem of bribery as a way of life.

Today, in many churches, testimony is greeted with applause. We need to think carefully about what we are saying through the applause and to evaluate whether this is the most effective and helpful way to draw the testimony to a close. On very many occasions it may be more appropriate for the leader or the church to pray in response to the testimony. It may be a prayer of praise or thanksgiving for what God has done or it may be a prayer asking for God's continued blessing on the life of the brother or sister in Christ.

Preaching

We have already discussed at some length the relationship of worship and preaching but it is probably helpful to reinforce the point that preaching is one of the keys to creating worship that touches people's lives. Worship and preaching work together in that the worship prepares the ground for the hearing of God's Word and then applies the message and reinforces the truths in the people's lives.

Much of course depends on the preacher. All too often preaching is boring and irrelevant, teaching God's Word in a dry, academic way which neither attracts the hearer nor touches lives. Preaching must not only convey biblical truth in a way that is attractive and memorable but it must relate those truths to our daily lives. After the preaching the worship leader should pick up the theme of the message and continue to apply its truth to the people's lives with suitable songs or prayers of response.

Individual Participation

So far we have considered how worship as a whole should engage with or participate in the daily lives of the congregation. In this section we are going to think about the individual contribution of members. One of the applications of Paul's metaphor of the Body of Christ is that every member of the body has individual gifts to be contributed for the common good[15]. This is particularly true in the area of worship. We need to encourage members to use their gifts to the full for the benefit of all. This involves discovering the members' gifts and then encouraging their use.

A Variety of Contributions

It needs to be recognised that there are a wide variety of individual contributions and all are of value. Sometimes there may be a tendency to value one contribution above another, but we do so at our peril. On one occasion nearly everyone had arrived for the worship service. The preacher, the worship leader, the musicians, the ushers, the Sunday

---

[15] 1 Cor 12:7-11

School teachers and the congregation, but the service couldn't begin. Why not? The key-holder was late and everyone was locked out of the building! Ranked according to importance the key-holder may not rate very high compared to others such as the preacher or worship leader, but yet his presence and contribution is vital!

Who then are some of the people who can make contributions to the worship service apart from the leader and preacher? A brief exemplary list is provided below:

- Greeters/ ushers/ stewards/ treasurer
- Singers (choir)/ musicians/ dancers
- Readers/ prayer leaders
- Announcers
- PA system and multi-media technician
- Caterers/ caretakers/ cleaners/ flower-arrangers

It is probably worthwhile to make a few specific comments on some of these contributions but all of them are vital for the smooth running of the service. In small churches one or two people may be responsible for several aspects, but as far as possible the jobs should be shared out to involve as many members as feasible. A responsible person should be in charge of each section, training should be arranged (if necessary) and appropriate schedules prepared to timetable individual involvement. The member's contribution should be valued and acknowledged, not taken for granted.

Greeters, Ushers and Stewards

Different churches use a variety of terms such as greeter, usher or steward, but what we are talking about here is those who are the first point of contact with members and newcomers coming to worship. This is such a vital role that many pastors and church leaders may also take part in this welcoming process that sets the tone for the subsequent worship experience. Greeters need to have a friendly, welcoming personality that makes people feel wanted and at home in the worship.

The role of the greeter may vary from church to church, but it essentially involves welcoming, assisting and equipping the worshipper

Participation

with any bulletin, books or worship materials. The greeter should know members by name and should be able to recognise a stranger or newcomer. The newcomer needs to be given special attention, provided with a welcome pack[16] or address card and introduced to the pastor, leaders or other church members. Someone should accompany newcomers into the worship centre, help them to find a seat [17] and perhaps sit with them.

If it is a large church or a crowded one people may need to be on duty in the worship centre assisting people to find a seat and encouraging people to sit nearer the front and closer to one another. The ushers or stewards may also be involved during and after the service. During the service they may be responsible for taking up the offering or in distributing communion elements[18]. After the service it may involve, together with the treasurer, counting and recording the offering.

Singers, Musicians and Dancers

There is tremendous potential for members to use their singing, musical and dancing skills in the worship. Singers may take part in solo or choir items or as a support to the worship leader[19]. If song presentations are made they should be relevant to the theme of the worship and not

---

[16] It is very helpful for newcomers if some basic information is prepared about the church and its activities to be given to newcomers. This information will include: names and contact for the pastor and church leaders; times of services and other activities such as cell groups or Sunday School *etc* ; information such as the Mission statement or vision of the church.

[17] This is not as easy as it might seem. As a newcomer you may have no indication as to where you are supposed to or allowed to sit. Long time members may have their favourite seats or possibly a section of the seating is reserved for the children or mothers with babies and so on.

[18] In other traditions this may be the role of the deacons, elders or readers.

[19] Unfortunately, in the contemporary worship scene, especially with the use of keyboards and music groups, it has become almost an imperative that the worship leader has a good solo singing voice. This is necessary as often the music group fails to give a clear lead to the congregation and it is the worship leader who must introduce the songs. The downside of this is that worship leaders may be selected for their musical (singing) ability rather than their spirituality and depth of understanding of worship. A way around this problem is the use of a back-up singer who can assist the worship leader to lead the introductions of the songs. The singer need not be on stage but could be in the front row of the congregation.

simply an item of entertainment. A whole range of musical instruments can be used in the worship, but musicians need to work together as a team, be prepared to practise together and recognise that they are the servants of the congregation – sometimes the singing might benefit from less rather than more accompaniment.

Dance is a relative newcomer on the scene[20]. Very common in Malaysia is the *Rebana* or tambourine dance. This normally involves a team of dancers dancing as an accompaniment to the praise songs. This can be very artistic, add colour and exuberance to the worship. However, the significance of the tambourine dancing is rarely explained so that it does little to feed the mind of the worshipper. A related form is dramatic or interpretive dance. This might accompany song, music or even the reading of the Scriptures and acts out the story or interprets some Christian truth. It can be extremely moving and helpful, touching the heart and challenging the mind.

Drama is another art form that needs to be welcomed into our worship. The Christian message is dramatic and can helpfully be acted out. Sometimes drama might be used to introduce or illustrate the preaching, or to bring home the meaning of a part of the worship. At one Good Friday service the preacher used drama to bring home the impact of Jesus' trial. The trial was taking place at the front of the church and the congregation was acting the part of the crowd who waited to hear the verdict. As Pilate asked the crowd who did they want released, Jesus or Barabbas, a team of actors moved through the congregation whispering and urging the name Barabbas. So powerful was the dramatic impact that before long almost the whole congregation were irresistibly calling out "Barabbas!" And not long after saying of Jesus, "Crucify Him!"

Bible Readers

It is sometimes assumed that if you can read, then automatically you can read the Scriptures in front of the congregation. Nothing could be further from the truth. To read well in public is a skill to be learned and training and practice are vital. The public reading of the Scriptures should be one of the highlights of the worship service – a Bible reading

---

[20] Some background to the use of dance in worship is given in Boschman (1994) pp 47-65.

Participation

read well can be inspirational and challenging. Furthermore, reading the Bible in the worship service as well as leading prayers should be the starting point for those thinking of becoming worship leaders.

Although there is no substitute for experience and practical training on site[21] there are some specific guidelines that can be given. First of all prepare the reading well. This means that the reader needs to have the passage a few days in advance. Preparation involves reading the text through several times, making sure how to pronounce each word – if there are difficult biblical names, seek help. If no one else knows how to pronounce the names, decide on a likely possibility and say it with confidence.

As you read through the passage make sure you understand the passage and can read it with understanding. Try to get the *feel* of the reading so that you can read with expression. Check the Bible version to be used and make sure you practise with the correct translation. If the print is too small you may be able to photocopy a larger print version or even print the passage directly from a Bible software[22]. Prepare a very brief (two or three sentence) introduction to the Bible passage. On the day get to church early and practise standing behind the lectern, making sure that you can see the text of the Bible passage and use the microphone. Sit near the front so that you can move forward quickly and easily to read.

Where possible[23], try to be in position to read as soon as the time allocated arrives. Begin the reading by clearly and slowly announcing the passage. An example of a possible introduction is outlined below:

> Reader: The New Testament reading is taken from the Gospel of Luke chapter 14, beginning to read at verse 25.

---

[21] It is important that the reader knows how to use a microphone (if one is used) and how to speak in a way that can be clearly heard. This is best practised in the worship centre with someone who can provide some feedback.

[22] If you are printing for public reading from a lectern, then around a 16pt font is a good size for most people.

[23] For example, if there is a song or hymn before the reading, move to the lectern during the singing of the final verse or chorus so that you are ready to announce the reading.

(*Brief introduction*) At a time when Jesus was very popular, and huge crowds were following Him, He reminds them of the true cost of discipleship.
The Gospel of Luke chapter 14, verse 25.
(*Reading*) 'Large crowds were travelling with Jesus ...'
(*Ending*) This is the Word of the Lord.

People: **Thanks be to God!**

The actual wording will depend on the tradition of the church, but in addition to reading the Bible passage there needs to be a brief introduction and an ending. It is inappropriate to end the reading by shutting the Bible and hastily returning to your seat. At the close of the passage some brief concluding statement needs to be made. It could simply be 'Amen' or 'Here ends the first Scripture reading' or 'Thanks be to God for the reading of His Word' or some other format or response which indicates that the reading has ended.

During the reading the reader should try, from time to time, to look at the congregation and not keep her head in the Bible. The reading should be clear and unhurried, with pauses, where appropriate, to bring out the powerful drama of the text. After the reading the reader returns calmly to her place and sits down and the worship flows on.

Prayer Leaders

Another way in which individuals can participate is through leading the intercessory prayers. This need not be the role of the worship leader. Sometimes the intercessory prayers may be conducted by the pastor or, alternatively, by a member of the congregation who has a burden for prayer ministry and intercession. Intercessory prayers should be prepared so that the church is faithful in its prayer support for people – those within the church, those sent out by the church and those in the wider world. Details of ways of praying and intercessory prayer have already been discussed and so will not be elaborated further here.

Announcers

Probably announcements are the low point of many worship services. Notices given after the preaching may erase any lasting challenge, or, if at the beginning of the service, may do little to create a worshipful

Participation

atmosphere. It is imperative that the announcements are seen as a critical part of the worship and not as an unimportant extra. They should add to the worship and not detract from it.

Probably the pastor, or one of the church leaders, who have a good rapport with the congregation and can make the announcements come alive, should give the announcements regularly. Notices should be kept to a minimum but will probably include:

- A welcome – especially to any newcomers[24] or maybe the visiting preacher.
- Important news about the church family[25].
- Brief report about recent church activities[26].
- Encouragement to be involved in church projects[27].

---

[24] This could helpfully be a welcome by name if the greeters have done their work and provided the information to the announcer. But avoid embarrassing people; not everyone likes to stand up in front of the crowd. Helpful comments could be: "We would like to welcome in our midst Mr and Mrs A friends of ..."; or, "We are delighted to welcome Mary Brown to our worship. Mary has just moved into the area and will be working at the local hospital..."; or, "We are thrilled to welcome back to the fellowship Anne and Robert who are our missionaries in Venezuela ...".

[25] Part of the role of the announcements is to encourage the members to feel that they are part of the Family of God. When something important happens, or is going to happen, to one of the congregation, then other members of the family need to be informed. This might be bereavement, an accident, a serious illness, or a wedding, a forthcoming baptism, a 100th birthday celebration or a promotion at work. The announcements can helpfully be tied in with intercessory prayer so that the church family are not only informed but join in prayer for their brothers and sisters in Christ. Minor details such as who donated the flowers, or how much offering was given the previous week can be limited to the notice sheet if required.

[26] This will not be a routine item but will be given occasionally to encourage the congregation. Such items might include, for example, the total amount of money given on a special Missions Gift Day or the harvest from a recent evangelistic campaign. The information is given not just to inform but also to encourage. For example, the brief report might be ended with a word of thanks to all those who gave, helped or prayed.

[27] Normally the details of the church activities, times, dates and meeting places will all be detailed in the notice sheet or bulletin. These do not need repeating. People cannot remember dates and times given orally or something happening several weeks in advance. Limit oral calendar announcements to: today, this evening, on Friday night, next Sunday *etc*. What is important is to encourage people to participate or be involved in the activities.

- Leadership decisions[28].
- Invitation[29]

Of course not all the above will be necessary each week. Detailed information should be given in the notice sheet. Names of people on duty can be summarised in the bulletin or church notice board and if necessary reminded by the church secretary.

The church should have a policy of not giving out last minute notices except in a real emergency – such as, 'the building is on fire!' If activities are really important people will soon learn the discipline of providing the information in advance. There is nothing worse than a succession of scraps of paper being hurriedly past to the front, followed by a pause as the announcer tries to decipher the scrawled script and the subsequent dialogue with the informant such as: – "Is it *this* Friday you mean?" "Is it just for young children or can the youth come too?"

Many churches use OHPs for projecting the worship songs but rarely for announcements. If you are serious in trying to encourage people to participate, consider making your announcement visual. A projected picture of the church family enjoying themselves at a seaside resort, mountain retreat or guesthouse might be a more effective advertisement for the forthcoming church camp than a lot of words. The OHP can also be used to make 'silent' announcements. For example, the worshippers might be greeted by a slide with a suitable picture and the wording – 'Welcome to our service. Please prepare yourself for worship in silent prayer.'

Summary

There are a wide variety of opportunities for members to make individual contributions to the corporate worship. However, it is important to try and match individual gifts with the task and responsibility. All contributions are valuable but some are better suited 'up-front' whereas others can best contribute working behind the

---

[28] It is important to update the members about important decisions or appointments made by the church leadership to encourage membership support.

[29] Finally there may be an invitation for newcomers or the whole church family to stay back for refreshments and fellowship after the worship.

Participation

scenes. Some of the more practical and technical contributions will be discussed briefly in a subsequent chapter.

Corporate Participation

So far we have discussed how worship should engage with the life and experience of each church member. We have also thought how individuals can participate through a personal contribution. However, the most important aspect of participation in corporate worship is the involvement of the whole worshipping body. The worshippers are not onlookers but rather essential members of the cast in the enacted drama of worship. Without the actors there can be no play, without the congregation there can be no corporate worship.

The most important role of the worship leader is to prepare and lead worship in a way that enables the whole congregation to worship. Some of the ways of doing this have already been touched on in the chapters on prayer and praise, but it is worth looking at this important topic in a little more detail. In the section that follows we will examine various corporate activities.

Singing

Perhaps the most widely used corporate activity is song. Singing was evidently an important part of the worship life of the early Christians[30]. This is something that has the potential to unite the whole congregation in worship. But it may not. Various important factors are considered below which need to be taken into account.

Music

Whether or not the song is accompanied it is inherently musical – there is a tune, there is a harmony. Music is something very special in that it interacts with our being in a way that the simple spoken word does not. Music is especially important in enabling us to express feeling and

---

[30] There are abundant references to psalms, hymns and singing within the worship of the New Testament Church. See, for example: Mat 26:30; Mk 14:26; Acts 16:25; 1 Cor.14:15,26; Eph 5:19; Col 3:16; James 5:15. Certain passages such as: Luke 1:46-55; 2:29-32; Phil.2:6-11 may have actually been the text of early Christian hymns.

emotion. Beautiful, tender music can move us to tears; triumphant, expressive music can make us feel joyful and help us reach out to God in praise.

Music is powerful and is rightly a part of our worship. This was vividly brought home to me when I led a service in a residential home for elderly people, many of them in their eighties and nineties. There was one elderly lady who had had a stroke that had affected her so that she could no longer talk or respond verbally in conversation. However, when we sang together one of the traditional hymns that she had known since a child she could sing! And sing she did! Music was the key to unlock her mind and enable her to worship her Lord.

Music is important because it helps to maintain the balance of our worship. For example, a musical accompaniment to a hymn helps us to feel or experience our expression of worship, whilst the words are feeding our minds, and our voices and bodies are articulating our praises.

Variety

Paul urges the Christians in Ephesus:
> "Speak to one another with psalms, hymns and spiritual songs. Sing and make music in your heart to the Lord, always giving thanks to God the Father for everything, in the name of our Lord Jesus Christ." (Eph 5:19,20)

Although the precise difference between psalms, hymns and spiritual songs is not clear, it certainly suggests variety[31]. This variety can helpfully be reflected in our contemporary worship. For example, the congregation can be involved in singing: hymns, choruses, psalms, prayers, and responses[32]. Sometimes singing something that we normally say together such as the Lord's Prayer or maybe the Apostle's Creed can generate a whole new understanding and appreciation of something that may have become routine.

---

[31] It is sometimes suggested that psalms refer to the OT compositions, hymns to recent Christian writings and 'spiritual songs' to spontaneous inspiration by the Holy Spirit, or 'singing in the Spirit' (1 Cor 14:15), but it is by no means certain.

[32] In some churches affected by the Charismatic renewal the congregation may sing in 'tongues'. This is normally unaccompanied spontaneous singing – the musical version of speaking in tongues. It can be a most moving and beautiful experience.

Participation　　　　　　　　　　　　　　　　　　　　　　　　　　　　125

There is also a wide variety in songs and hymns available for worship and no reason why the local church should not write its own. Care needs to be exercised in the choice of hymns or songs so that the leader does not simply choose his or her favourites or those that are easy to flow together musically[33].

Hymns

Many of the traditional hymns are very rich in theology and were in part designed to teach believers doctrine as well as to enable worship. For example, the magnificent Wesleyan Christmas hymn, *Hark! the Herald-Angels Sing* explains line by line the significance of the newborn child whom we celebrate at Christmas. Thus, the second verse, reproduced below, is a profound exposition of the deity of Christ[34] and the meaning of the incarnation:

>Christ, by highest heaven adored,
>Christ, the everlasting Lord,
>Late in time behold Him come,
>Offspring of a virgin's womb.
>Veiled in flesh the Godhead see!
>Hail the incarnate Deity!
>Pleased as man with man to dwell,
>Jesus our Immanuel.

Such hymns are invaluable for proclaiming and confirming what Christians believe.

The difficulty of course is that we live in an age of communication English with an emphasis on simplicity and directness, rather than depth. As a consequence, much of the rich language of past generations of Christian hymn-writers has become almost incomprehensible to

---

[33] One common trend where there is an extended section of worship songs is to sing them seamlessly without a break between songs. Songs are sometimes chosen on the basis that they are in the same key making the sequence easier to play. This may override the importance of the words or the theme that is being addressed.

[34] The divine nature of Christ is detailed by Wesley's references to: the heavenly worship accorded Him; His titles as 'everlasting Lord' and 'Immanuel'; and the bald statements that we see the 'Godhead' and the 'incarnate deity' in the baby of Bethlehem.

many in this modern age. This poses a dilemma. Should we completely abandon the heritage of the past in deference to the needs of the younger generations, or should we continue to use hymns so as to avoid marginalizing the senior members of the church? As always the answer lies in seeking a balanced response. This may necessitate explaining and drawing attention to the meaning of more obscure language.

There are of course modern hymn-writers who use the idiom of today's world, but few can match the theology of the Wesleys or Luther.

Short Choruses

Modern choruses are usually paradigms of simplicity and are normally designed to help us express our feelings for God and for one another. For example the chorus:[35]

> Jesus, Jesus, Jesus, your love has melted my heart,
> Jesus, Jesus, Jesus, your love has melted my heart.

is an articulation of how we feel about what God has done in our lives. In many ways choruses such as these should not be separated from the accompanying music, since, although the words alone may seem trite, taken together with an evocative tune, the overall effect may be very powerful. Another simple but very moving chorus that enables us to express our worship has the lyric:[36]

> Father, we adore You,
> Lay our lives before You,
> How we love You.

The above chorus is Trinitarian in form as subsequent verses use the name Jesus and then Spirit. Many choruses may rightly be called *Scripture Choruses*, since their words are derived from the Bible. An example of this is the chorus based on 1 Peter 2:9:[37]

> Come and praise him, royal priesthood,
> Come and worship, holy nation,
> Worship Jesus our Redeemer,
> He is precious, King of glory.

---

[35] Songs of Fellowship (1991) 294

[36] Songs of Fellowship (1991) 99

[37] Songs of Fellowship (1991) 65

Participation

The benefit of using such choruses is that as they are learnt, so the Scriptures are being memorized.

Quite apart from providing variety, there are two further reasons for making use of choruses. Firstly, they are very helpful for those who cannot read or are partially sighted[38]. Short choruses, especially if sung two or three times, are quickly memorized and enable these special groupings to take full part in the worship. Secondly, if choruses are known by heart, then they can be used spontaneously, as in a time of open prayer or praise. Furthermore, freed from holding a book, worshippers may more easily use their hands in acts of worship.

Memory

Hymns and choruses speak to us through the words we express and the music that moves and stirs us. But there is another way in which they enable our participation in worship and that is through evoking memories. Earlier in this chapter we thought about the therapeutic power of music in the elderly and maybe this is related to the memory.

As we sing a familiar tune it will awaken our memory and remind us, maybe only subconsciously, of earlier worship occasions when we have sung that hymn. The hymn has a hidden resonance with our inner being.[39] This has the potential to enrich our worship although of course it may only cause us to feel nostalgic[40], or on occasions be a negative experience.[41] As we sing, the many positive worship experiences of the past, and the remembered links with fellow believers, will reinforce our present day worship and make it a much richer experience. This is probably one of the reasons that many older Christians find singing modern hymns and choruses such a barren worship experience. There

---

[38] This includes both the young who have not yet learnt to read and the old who may not be able to see. But note, simple choruses may not necessarily be suitable for children if they are based on adult or abstract ideas.

[39] Something of the depth of this feeling is perhaps captured in the Psalmist's longing for the worship in Jerusalem as expressed in Ps 42:4.

[40] For example, a hymn sung on your wedding day or a favourite hymn of a deceased loved one.

[41] For example, singing of a hymn that was often sung in school assemblies might have a negative effect if school had been a bad experience and assemblies boring.

are no positive worship memories and instead they have to struggle with new and seemingly difficult tunes and the feeling of awkwardness in expressing their feelings to God.

Corporate Singing

The one thing that cannot be over-stressed is that the singing needs to be *corporate*. Solo and choir items have a place in worship, but the most important choir is the congregation. Great care must be taken to ensure that the music, choir or singers lead, accompany and encourage the congregation to sing. All too often music groups and amplified singers dominate the singing and render the congregation superfluous. Whereas the people may need an initial lead, subsequently it should be the congregation who are in the foreground, otherwise the people become audience rather than worshippers.

If congregational singing is taken seriously then there may need to be some training, especially when singing new songs for the first time. It is perhaps unreasonable to expect the whole congregation to come on another occasion to practise singing, but it is possible to use a few minutes before the start of the worship service to teach new tunes or alternative ways of singing. One of the riches of the Methodist tradition has been congregational singing. Not only do many congregations sing well and with enthusiasm but they can also sing in choral parts so that the congregation works together as one whole choir. This is a tradition to be valued and learnt from.

The modern age, especially in the West, is an age that stresses the importance of the individual rather than the community. Often, modern worship songs reflect this tendency in their lyrics. It is probably fair to say that the majority of contemporary worship songs speak with the voice of the individual – I, me and my. Thus we tell God that 'I love You', 'I worship You', 'I bow down before You' or 'I offer my life to You'. All these are perfectly legitimate personal responses to God, but they are not corporate! When we worship together with our brothers and sisters in Christ, although sometimes we are called to make a personal response to God, usually we should be worshipping with the voice of the body of Christ – we, us and our. This needs to be considered when selecting worship songs.

Responsive Readings

Not all of us have good singing voices, and although we may take pleasure in hearing beautiful singing, yet we may feel we cannot fully participate. Another approach to enabling the participation of the congregation is through responsive readings. Many of the psalms can be used as effective means of worship, especially for: praise[42], confession[43], the presence of God[44], and thanksgiving[45]. Some hymnbooks include a selection of psalms edited as responsive readings, but alternatively one can use a common version of the Bible or even hymns or choruses. The latter may be very useful where the words are very beautiful or appropriate to the occasion but the tune unknown or too difficult to sing.

Even with the use of responsive readings there is potential for variety. The readings can be read in unison or in parts. The parts in turn can be taken by: the leader and the congregation; men responding to women; or one half of the congregation with the other half. As a further variation the two halves of the congregation can be asked to turn to face one another to get the full *feel* of the responsive nature of the psalms. The readings may be carried out kneeling, seated or standing. Probably praise psalms are most expressive when standing and confession psalms when kneeling. Every effort should be made to bring life into the responsive readings and to reflect something of the fervour of the psalmist. On some occasions it may be helpful for the leader to lead from the body of the congregation so that a greater sense of intimacy may be expressed.

Expressions of Fellowship

Increasingly, contemporary worship is alive to the need for expressions of fellowship and the recognition that we are truly brothers and sisters in one family and united to Christ as members of one body. Such expressions are particularly appropriate in services such as the

---

[42] See, for example: Psalm 95, 96, 98, 100, 145-148
[43] See Psalm 51, 139
[44] Psalm 46
[45] Psalm 107, 118

celebration of the Lord's Supper where we gather together around the Lord's Table and partake of the one loaf. The significance of these events can be further heightened by seating arrangements where the Table is in the centre of the congregation and where a whole loaf is used as the symbol of the one body.[46]

However, even within the usual worship service, it is possible to have powerful expressions of fellowship and oneness, and recognition that we are all part of the Body of Christ. One way is through saying the words of the Grace to one another. Instead of having our eyes shut, eye contact is made with our sisters and brothers in the congregation as we pray for them. Other expressions might include passing the Peace where members join hands and say: "The peace of the Lord be with you", whereupon, the recipient replies: "And with you!". Alternatively, on Easter Sunday one might use the following greeting: "Christ is risen!" with the response, "He is risen indeed!"

Another approach is to use a chorus as an opportunity for the congregation to move from their seats in order to greet one another. Suitable choruses include ones with the following first lines:

"Bind us together, Lord..."[47]
"I love you with the love of the Lord..."[48]
"Jesus stand among us...."[49]
"Let there be love shared among us..."[50]

It helps if the chorus is known by heart as then eye contact can be made and hands used for grasping other hands.

Expressions of fellowship are very difficult to introduce for the first time and the leader needs to be sensitive to the atmosphere and feelings within the congregation. The leader needs to be aware that the time is

---

[46] Often the sacrament of Holy Communion can be celebrated in a very individualistic way, whereas, although it has a personal meaning for all who take part, it should be the highlight of corporate worship. See 1 Cor 10:16,17

[47] Songs of Fellowship (1991) 43

[48] Songs of Fellowship (1991) 228

[49] Songs of Fellowship (1991) 303

[50] Songs of Fellowship (1991) 329

right for such expression. Instructions must be clearly given to explain what is intended and it is helpful to lead by example. Thus if members of the congregation are to move around the church greeting one another, then the leader should be among the first to do so. Timing within the service is also important – often an act of fellowship may be a response to the message or part of the conclusion of the service.

The Offering

The finance of the local church is clearly the responsibility of the whole membership and so the offering should be an act of worship that involves full corporate participation. Unfortunately, the importance of our giving as worship is frequently not understood. This is illustrated by the casual attitude towards this aspect of worship; for example, the offering is often not located at an appropriate point in the worship, or is carelessly introduced as 'the collection' – which implies now is the time for members to pay their dues or membership fee! The significance of the offering is completely destroyed when it is seen as an occasion for chatting by the congregation, or notice giving by the leader.

It is imperative that the offering be seen as an integral part of the worship and not as a fund-raising interlude. As such, the time for giving tithes and offerings must be carefully and clearly introduced. An introduction such as: "We will now continue to worship the Lord in the giving of our offerings." might be appropriate. If necessary, specify what the money is to be used for – this is relevant in the case of giving for special purposes. It is important to decide what will happen while the offerings are being given – a time of silence, music being played, or a hymn being sung. The leader should try and encourage the congregation to see the giving of offerings as an integral part of the worship and as symbolic of the giving of their lives to God.

If the actual process of giving seems to take a disproportionate amount of time, then it may be helpful to provide additional offering bags and employ more stewards. When all the offerings have been given, there will normally be an opportunity to dedicate the money and ourselves to the Lord in an offering prayer or response. A good model of such a prayer may be found in David's prayer of dedication for the offerings given towards the building of the Temple[51]. Alternatively, a response such as the following may be appropriate:

> Leader: *All things come from You, O Lord!*
> People: **And of Your own we have given You!**

Each church needs to create its own meaningful style of giving to the Lord that encourages offering as an act of worship. In some churches the offering box is placed at the door so that members can give discreetly as they enter and visitors are not pressurised to give. However, even with this tradition the offerings should be brought to the front at some point and symbolically offered to God with prayer as a reminder that offering is worship.

Summary

We have seen in detail that corporate worship involves full participation. This means essentially three things. Firstly, worship should touch and *participate* in our daily lives. As disciples of Christ worship should relate to our daily experience and thus enrich our lives, work and witness. Secondly, in worship we *participate* as individuals, contributing our personal gifts and skills. Thirdly, worship should involve the *participation* of the whole body of Christ. Such *participation* can be facilitated through various aspects of worship, specifically in: prayer, singing, responsive readings, acts of fellowship and offerings.

---

[51] 1 Chr 29:10-20

8 – Place

The place of worship has a vital influence on the conduct and outcome of worship. To worship on a mountain top or beside the sea can be an exhilarating experience as one marvels at the wonder of God's creation – it can, though, be difficult for the preacher who struggles to be heard amidst the distractions of the elements and hard on the congregation if surprised by a sudden rain storm! For this reason most worship is conducted in some kind of shelter that protects from the elements and to some extent shuts out distractions.[1] Although the starting point is a shelter, most church buildings are designed as a place that enables people to meet together and is conducive to worship. Ultimately, many buildings become more than that, they become a sanctuary or holy place specially set aside for worship.[2]

The Role of Buildings in Worship

In the previous chapter the point has been clearly made that the biblical understanding of Church is not a building but the people of God. We are *together* God's Temple[3] and where two or three believers are

---

[1] The precise nature of the shelter obviously depends on the environment and requirements. In rural areas in the tropics little more than a roof is required to protect from sun and rain – open sided buildings provide ventilation and easy movement of people. When the church moves to the town, other considerations such as security, traffic noise and noise disturbance to other people usually require more enclosed buildings of brick or concrete. In cold European climates an enclosed building is also required for warmth.

[2] This was one of the problems confronting John Wesley in the 18th Century. He felt called by God to preach the Gospel to the vast numbers of people in Britain who never attended worship services. However, at that time, it was considered improper to preach outside of consecrated church buildings. The Church authorities were scandalised that John Wesley, an Anglican priest, would preach God's holy word in public places and in the open air.

[3] 1 Cor 3:16, 6:19

gathered in Christ's name, He is present in the midst.[4] The prime role of the building is thus to house the worshippers rather than God who is worshipped. It is God's people who are being built as living stones into a holy temple – a centre for God's praise. The building is not a temple[5] but rather a shelter for God's people who are to become His temple.

With this understanding we shall realise that the prime function of the building or place of worship is to house God's people and to act as meeting place, shelter and worship centre.

A Meeting Place

Historically the very first proclamations of the Christian message have taken place where people could easily gather and meet together. It might have been a market place, or at a crossroads, a meeting hall or an amphitheatre, a hillside or a riverside. However, whereas the Gospel is proclaimed publicly, worship has generally tended to take place in more secluded surroundings.

New Testament meeting places

Although, to begin with, the Jewish Christians continued to worship in the Temple and synagogues[6], yet the believers also met to worship and fellowship in a number of other places. For example, the central aspect of Christian worship, the Lord's Supper, was conducted in rented rooms[7] and believers' homes.[8] Homes were also used for prayer meetings and worship.[9] It is also evident, from the wording of Paul's

---

[4] Mat 18:20

[5] This truth is clearly apparent in Paul's proclamation in Athens that: 'The God who made the world and everything in it is the Lord of heaven and earth and does not live in temples built by hands.' (Acts 17:24)

[6] Acts 2:46

[7] Acts 1:13

[8] Acts 2:46

[9] Acts 12:12

greetings in his letters, that churches met in the homes of individuals such as Priscilla and Aquila.[10]

What is quite evident is that in the first century there were no purpose-built church buildings. The Christians met wherever they could conveniently gather together in reasonable comfort and safety. In some countries today churches still find it necessary to meet in homes, or rented halls, since new church buildings are not permitted.[11] Thus many Christians, especially in urban centres in the newly developing world, worship in temporary accommodation[12] – a home, a shop-house, a warehouse, a hotel, or a school.

Basic Criteria

Very often we may not have too much say in the choice of building that is used for the meeting place of the church; rather we make use of what we have inherited or what is available. But it is worth considering just very briefly what makes for a suitable meeting place.

The first requirement is that it must be *accessible*. In a rural setting this may mean it is located in the village within walking distance of homes or, in the town, preferably near to some means of public transport or easily accessible by car, and with adequate parking facilities. It's a bonus if the building is prominently situated so as to be easily found. Today, accessible also means having ramps or access for those who use wheel chairs or have problems with mobility.

The second requirement is that it should be *welcoming*. What this means depends to some extent on those whom you are encouraging to come and join you. For many who are not particularly religious a church building can be a scary or off-putting place and not their choice of a meeting place. This may be the advantage of meeting in a home, or

---

[10] Rom 16:5, 1 Cor 16:19

[11] This is true, for example, in many Islamic and Communist countries.

[12] It is perhaps a reminder that as Christians we are a pilgrim people, a people on the move. We are going places and so like the Israelites in the wilderness we do not have a permanent place of stay. Temporary or rented accommodation also provides flexibility against future needs. The church can move as it grows.

in the alternative worship scene in a coffee bar style premises or even a public house.[13]

Nowadays some traditional buildings in Britain are being modified with a glass frontage. This provides not only natural lighting but makes the building more open to outsiders.

Welcoming relates not just to the type of premises but also its environment and décor. The building needs to be clearly identified as a meeting place with an appropriate sign making clear who is welcome, for what purpose and when. The meeting place and its surroundings need to be neat and clean and well cared for. The entrance should be clearly marked and the interior décor should be bright and welcoming. All the fixtures, fittings and furnishings should be in a good state of repair, and a prominent notice board containing only current[14] and well prepared notices! All of this comprises a vital ministry in the church.

All too often our buildings and their surroundings are uncared for and loudly proclaim the message: 'This is a depressing place – enter at your peril!' The peeling paint, cracked windows, unkempt gardens and illegible notice board of the British housing estate church building proclaim the same message as the waist-high grass, litter-strewn surroundings and mud-caked entrance of a Sabah village church building. This place is uncared for, we are dying – do you care to join us?

A Shelter

The building where the church gathers is usually more than just a meeting place, it is also a shelter. At its most primitive it may be a large

---

[13] Of course, the coffee bar format is not completely new – I well remember in the sixties in Manchester being involved in the outreach of the *Catacombs*, an underground coffee bar style front for evangelism.

[14] I never ceased to be amazed by how many notice boards are covered with notices advertising past events – sometimes even dating back a year or more. There should be an individual responsible for looking after the notice board and all notices should be marked with a discrete take down date.

Place

tree[15] that shelters the worshippers from the elements, but usually it will be some kind of building. The essential purpose of the shelter is to provide protection – protection from the heat or the cold, from rain or snow, from distractions and noise, from enemies or thieves. As the church becomes materially richer so the shelter will become more sophisticated in order to cater for the comfort of the members and to provide security for a growing number of possessions.

Physical comfort and safety

Physical comfort also implies that care needs to be given to aspects such as seating[16], heating, air-conditioning or ventilation of the centre.[17] Fire safety is also a very important consideration, especially in countries where fire regulations are not rigidly enforced. There need to be adequate exits, smoke detectors and fire extinguishers to deal with small fires.

Basic facilities

In addition to the worship centre, which we will discuss shortly, the building can helpfully be equipped with facilities such as: toilets and washroom; a small kitchen[18]; an office[19]; a store-place and one or more small meeting rooms.[20] In many ways a house provides a good approximation to this description and is a good starting point for a church. All of the above facilities are the basic requirements to house

---

[15] In the early Seventies I sometimes taught a Sunday School class on a Rubber Estate near Kuala Lumpur under the cool shade of a large tree. It was often cooler than the corrugated iron roofed alternative.

[16] Needs, of course, are variable, ranging from sitting on the floor, to benches, pews or individual seats. For very elderly or infirm people chairs with arm rests are a great help for sitting down and standing up.

[17] Heating or cooling can be very expensive. A good design of building and appropriate size for the congregation can help to minimise the costs. In tropical climates building designs that permit natural ventilation, together with roof insulation, can help greatly. Often natural materials are much cooler than the more convenient zinc roofing.

[18] To provide refreshments for fellowship meetings or after worship gatherings.

[19] For use by pastoral workers, secretary or treasurer.

[20] These can be used for prayer, counselling, fellowship or business meetings and, of course, children's work.

and serve the needs of the Christian community that meet and worship together.

The Worship Centre

The central activity of the Christian community is worship and thus the worship centre must be at the very heart of the design of the facilities. Clearly our theological understanding will influence the overall concept of worship centre. If we regard the centre as a temple where God dwells, then necessarily the building will be set apart, or consecrated, for worship alone. However, if we hold to the more biblical understanding that it is the people of God who form God's temple, then the building is a home for people and not God and this opens the way to a wider use for the worship centre. It also makes it possible to worship in what are usually considered as secular facilities such as schools, shops, offices, community centres and hotels.

Multi-purpose use

If we allow the possibility of multi-purpose use of the worship centre, then during the week the facilities might be used for educational, recreational or community activities. For example, in some countries it might be possible to use the premises as a kindergarten or for primary education or as a tuition centre. This provides a potential bridge to the local community, especially those who are sceptical of religion or the Church.

The plus side of a multi-purpose worship centre is that it provides for good stewardship of resources[21] and also makes it easier for outsiders to join the Church. For example, if fringe people have come to the building for community activities during the week, then the building is less mysterious and it is easier for them to join for Sunday worship services. Of course, there may also be those more traditionally minded who do not consider it to be a 'proper church' and hence stay away.

---

[21] To have an expensive premises (the cost of church buildings is usually in the realm of hundreds of thousands of pounds) that is used for only one or two hours a week is a very poor use of resources.

The main disadvantage of a multi-purpose centre is the sheer amount of additional work involved in rearranging the facilities. Unfortunately, designs rarely match the ingenuity of the theatre where the 'scene' can be changed by merely rotating the stage. At the very minimum, chairs need to be stacked and stored and equipment, books *etc* put away, and perhaps liturgical furnishings screened. However, this need not be an insurmountable problem if properly organised. If you need to use a lot of chairs it means you have a lot of members! Whereas for one person to stack 500 chairs is a mammoth task, for 500 persons to stack a chair each is hardly burdensome.

Basic requirements

If we set aside the question of consecrated single-use building or multi-purpose centre what are the things that make the place suitable for worship? Probably the most decisive factor is size.

To sit alone, silently worshipping within the cathedral-like structure of an ancient church building, isolated from the hurly-burly of the outside world, can be refreshing, like bathing in the cool pool of a waterfall after a strenuous hike. But to worship with a small congregation in the same building can be a difficult experience, as one struggles to create relationships with people who are isolated from the leader and one another by rows of empty pews. By contrast, to worship together with that same small congregation, packed together into someone's home, can provide an overwhelming sense of oneness and fellowship.

Appropriate size is of vital importance. For a good worship experience involving helpful interaction, encouraging singing and clear communication, the people must sit together, ideally in a space just large enough to comfortably accommodate everyone. Size is vital because it affects the personal dynamics, the acoustics and the comfort.[22] Small congregations in large buildings would do well to consider using an adjacent chapel or meeting room, or perhaps partitioning the main worship centre to reduce its size. The more

---

[22] To heat or air-condition a 1,000 seat building for a congregation of 20-30 people makes very little economic sense. A traditional stone church building in mid-winter will take hours to heat at great expense and still not be very comfortable.

compact the worship centre the easier it is for the people to fully participate in the worship and to become worshippers rather than spectators.

Aside from size, but related to it, the worship centre should have good acoustics and sight lines so that the leader or preacher and the congregation and musicians can be both seen and heard. The projection screen, if used, should be clearly visible to all the people, but should preferably not be the central or permanent feature of the décor.[23] The use of PA systems should be kept to a minimum – they should not be needed at all for congregations of 50 or less in appropriate sized meeting places.

Ideally, the layout of the worship centre should also be flexible so as to permit different styles of worship and worship activities. This necessarily means chairs rather than pews and preferably a moveable stage area rather than fixed furnishings. Such flexibility allows the possibility of the use of drama and dance, breaking up into small groups for discussion, fellowship or prayer, and various seating formations for the act of worship. For example, for the whole congregation to sit around the Lord's Table can be a very moving worship experience. To sit together in gently curved seating focussing on the worship leader or preacher rather than in straight lines can also provide a more homely feel that is conducive to corporate worship.

The Language of the Worship Centre

In principle, as Christians, we have unrestricted freedom to worship in any place.[24] However, this does not mean that 'any place will do' since the actual place of worship is important as it will influence our worship. This arises because we worship with our whole person: body and soul, heart and mind. Our surroundings inevitably affect how we feel, think and act and hence how we worship.

---

[23] Unless of course it is used creatively to display religious motifs or suitable backgrounds when not used for song lyrics. Alternatively a retractable screen can be used.

[24] In practice, of course, this freedom may be limited by the State or by local byelaws.

Place 141

As we have already suggested earlier in this chapter the building and its environment and the way it is maintained will speak to us. If it is clean, nicely decorated, well maintained and at a comfortable temperature, then it will convey a positive impression. If it is dirty, shabby, poorly maintained and freezing cold, or hot and stuffy, then it is hardly conducive to worship the King of kings.

Space and furnishing

However, aside from the general aesthetics, the whole layout of the worship centre and its furnishings speak to us about our worship. Thus White identifies the need for six distinct 'Liturgical spaces' within the traditional church building which include[25]:

- *Gathering space* – where worshippers meet together
- *Movement space* – which permits movements and processions as for example with weddings and funerals.
- *Congregational space* – where worshippers sit, kneel or stand to worship
- *Choir space* – area for choir/ musicians/ dance
- *Baptismal space* – where baptisms are conducted
- *Sanctuary space* – which is the area where the communion table or altar is located.

In many modern buildings, especially those that embrace the concept of multi-purpose use or were not purpose-built as a worship centre, the above spaces may not be so distinct and the layout of the worship centre is more flexible

For example, the gathering or fellowshipping space may not be a separate area as the people may actually meet together in the centre where the worship has just taken place. The choir space may overlap with the sanctuary space often as a stage or platform where the musicians, singers and worship leader are located. There may or may not be an altar or communion table – sometimes the communion

---

[25] White (2000) pp 86-89

elements are distributed from a simple table or trolley. Often there may be a space in front of the stage that is used by the dancers or as a gathering space for the congregation coming forward for prayer ministry or to receive the sacraments.

There are of course even more radical uses of liturgical space as described in Brian and Kevin Drapers' account of 'alternative' worship based on the use of the Labyrinth.[26] This is essentially a more individual experience than corporate worship and consequently the required space requirements are quite different, focussing on a personal journey through the worship centre rather than interactions with others.

Liturgical centres

In addition to the above 'liturgical spaces' White also identifies three or four[27] 'liturgical centres' that form the foci of worship in traditional church buildings. These include:

- *Baptismal font or pool* – for conducting the sacrament of baptism
- *Pulpit* – for reading and preaching the Word.
- *Altar-table* – for conducting the sacrament of Holy Communion

This summary of liturgical centres is deficient in the sense that it does not allow a focus for the leading of non-sacramental worship that is increasingly prominent in many Christian communities, especially those influenced by Charismatic renewal. The fourth suggested liturgical centre, the 'presider's chair', although of historical

---

[26] Draper (2000) 10-16. "... the Labyrinth is a walking meditation, based on an ancient form of pre-Christian ritual which was later adopted by Christians in their own worship... It looks like a maze, but in fact it is a circular path that leads you on an 'inward journey' to a central space, then out again... The Labyrinth symbolises our walk with God. You walk it slowly ... you are encouraged at various points to stop and think about a range of things..."

[27] White also identifies the 'presider's chair' as a fourth liturgical centre but is somewhat diffident about its contemporary significance. Until the fourth century it was apparently the centre from which the service was conducted and sermons preached.

significance, is hardly an adequate description for contemporary worship.

Furthermore, the practicalities of using multi-purpose buildings and non-purpose built premises, as well as changes in theological understanding and worship style, mean that the above list does not correspond with the real situation in many contemporary worship centres. In practice, the liturgical centres may be reduced to a simple lectern or even a music stand used for worship leading, reading the Scriptures, preaching and conducting the sacraments. A small table may be used to place the offering or to hold the communion elements, but the emphasis is on function and simplicity rather than symbolism.

Aside from these radical changes, many churches do not conform exactly to the pattern suggested above. In some churches, for example in the Methodist tradition, usually the pulpit is used for both leading the worship and preaching the Word. This perhaps arises from the long tradition of one person, the minister or local preacher, leading the service and preaching. In many traditions the 'lectern' is another focus for the worship that may be used for reading the Scriptures or perhaps leading the worship, whilst the pulpit is reserved for preaching.

Symbolism and meaning

Changes in liturgical centres or furnishings have not only occurred for practical reasons but also, to some extent, reflect the theological understanding of the worship.[28] Some aspects of this are briefly touched on in the paragraphs that follow,

Baptismal font or pool

The presence of a baptismal font or pool is a constant reminder of the Great Commission:

> "Therefore go and make disciples of all nations, baptizing them in the name of the Father and of the Son and of the Holy Spirit, and teaching

---

[28] In existing buildings, furnishings very often lag behind changes in theological understanding. For example, the Anglican cathedral in Kota Kinabalu has a very prominent altar that reflects an earlier Anglo-Catholic tradition. Today the Diocese is overwhelmingly Evangelical-Charismatic, but the altar remains.

them to obey everything I have commanded you. And surely I am with you always, to the very end of the age." (Mat 28:19,20)

It is evident from this text that it is the Church's responsibility not only to evangelise but to disciple and baptise.

Traditionally the font was placed at the main entrance of the church building to symbolise that through baptism we enter the Church. Practically, however, this is not a very helpful arrangement for corporate worship, as the baptism is taking place behind the congregation and it is difficult for the people to see and hear what is happening. For this reason many churches use a small mobile font – perhaps placed on the table at the front where it is clearly visible.

The choice of font or pool is also of great theological significance. A font will never be found in a Baptist church or in churches that accept only believer's baptism conducted by immersion. Practically, a baptismal pool is somewhat difficult to construct and to use[29], takes up considerable space and consequently is less often found in contemporary church buildings. Instead, baptisms are frequently conducted in rivers, the sea or local swimming pools. Whereas this allows baptism by immersion and the possibility or proclamation of faith in a public place, it removes baptism from the heart of corporate worship and is frequently attended by only the faithful few – leaders, friends and relatives rather than the whole Church family.

Baptism needs to be returned to the heart of worship. If baptism by immersion is considered essential, then ways need to be found to encourage the whole congregation to attend at an alternative venue, or more thought needs to be given to the construction of a baptismal pool.[30]

---

[29] The pool needs to be filled before the baptism, subsequently drained afterwards and kept safe from adventurous children.

[30] One of the most innovative designs I have come across is in the Roman Catholic Cathedral in Kota Kinabalu. The pool is constructed in the centre of the area in front of the altar rails. When not in use, the pool is covered by substantial mosaic tiles that can be safely walked upon. These are lifted to reveal tiled steps leading down to a very small pool – just enough for immersion – and then further steps leading up to the altar.

Pulpit

The pulpit primarily speaks of preaching or proclamation of the word of God. In some traditions, notably the *Presbyterians*, preaching is the prime focus of the worship service and this is emphasised with massive, centrally positioned pulpits in many of their historic church buildings. Both the sheer size[31] and the centrality of the position make the unmistakable statement that preaching is important. Unfortunately, sometimes the message can be misread to suppose that the preacher is important and that he or she is 'six foot above contradiction' – both metaphorically and literally.

In most other traditions, Anglican, Methodist, or Lutheran, the pulpit is normally offset to one side of the sanctuary to provide more of a balance between preaching and worship – particularly sacramental worship. However, in many modern multi-use buildings the pulpit has been relegated to history with the preacher making use of a small lectern. This does not mean that preaching is regarded as unimportant, far from it; rather it does mean that the preacher has even great freedom to pace the stage and dramatically act out the message. Furthermore, cordless microphones and audio-visual aids mediated via OHP or *Power Point* computer presentations provide additional means for the preacher to get across the message.

One benefit of removing the pulpit is to bring the preacher down to the level of the congregation and to create a more intimate relationship. On some occasions, especially where the pulpit is positioned a long way from the people, it is worth coming down to preach amidst the people. This is especially appropriate where the message is an intimate one and the congregation is small. However, there is just one reservation. In

---

The candidate comes from the congregation, through the sacrament of baptism to receive the sacrament of Holy Communion at the altar. The priest who conducts the baptism has a very small compartment alongside the pool where he can baptise but at the same time remain substantially dry. The pool uses the very minimum of water for immersion and the baptisms are carried out in full view of the congregation on the traditional Easter Saturday.

[31] Some of the pulpits are not only high but wide, allowing the preacher to pace up and down during delivery.

some churches the pulpit is equipped with a microphone that is attached to a 'hearing loop' designed to help those wearing a hearing aid to hear the leader and preacher more clearly. If you leave the pulpit, the effect is lost no matter how loudly you speak.

Altar-table

It needs to be realised that the terms 'altar' and 'table' have a completely different meaning both theologically and practically, although the two terms are often confused and sometimes used almost interchangeably. Confusion abounds since tables are often dressed up as altars and some subconsciously regard altars as tables. The practical difference is that a table has legs and is in principle readily moveable. An altar, on the other hand, is solid and may be made of stone or camouflaged with that appearance. A table is intended for a meal; an altar for a sacrifice and this is the symbolic message that is conveyed.

The altar is related to the Catholic understanding of the sacrament as sacrifice. The elements of bread and wine on consecration by the priest are considered to become the literal body and blood of Christ and are offered again by the priest on the altar as a sacrifice for our sins. The table, on the other hand, speaks of a fellowship meal. The bread and wine are now no longer the literal body and blood of Christ but the tokens of remembrance[32] of Christ's sacrifice, and symbols of the unity that we have together as members of the body of Christ.[33]

Part of the confusion is caused because many Christians do not have a clear understanding of the meaning of the sacrament. Many hold an intermediate position between the two extreme positions, believing that, although the sacrament is not a sacrifice, yet it is more than just remembrance. Through eating and drinking we are in a special way united with Christ and receive a blessing that is channelled through the sacrament. This understanding falls short of the more extreme position

---

[32] Luke 22:19
[33] 1 Cor 10:17

that our salvation is mediated through taking part in the renewed sacrifice of Christ.[34]

Those who view the sacrament as a token of remembrance but nevertheless use the vocabulary of the altar further confuse the situation. Thus people talk of holding an 'altar call' at an evangelistic rally or challenge people to lay their all on 'the altar'. Much of this is influenced by 19th Century revival hymns rich in these phrases.

Altars are usually found in consecrated church buildings and are usually located at a distance from the congregation. The altar speaks symbolically of sacrifice, of a holy and distant God, and may convey the idea that God is only accessible through the intermediacy of the priest. By contrast, the table may be close to the congregation or even in the midst. The table emphasises the intimacy of God's relationship with us and our relationship with other members of the body of Christ.

In much contemporary worship, especially in multi-use buildings, altars are much less in evidence. This may reflect as much practicality and ease of use as a conscious awareness of its significance. As has already been noted, a serving trolley may even replace the table with an emphasis on the elements being distributed to the congregation rather than the people coming to the table.

Christian symbols and decoration

Post Reformation Protestant churches in Britain were swept clean of most religious art and decorations to the extent that even many stained glass windows were destroyed. The motivation was positive in that it sought to remove anything that could become idolatrous or be worshipped in its own right[35], although the practice was frequently over

---

[34] The concept of the sacrament as sacrifice is difficult to justify in view of texts such as Heb 10:12 that imply that Christ as our High Priest has already: '... offered for all time one sacrifice for sins ...'.
[35] This is an understandable reaction to the state of the Roman Catholic Church in the 16th Century. Even today, many Roman Catholic churches have statuettes of Mary that are used by worshippers in intercessory prayer. Mary, and others of the saints, are seen as intermediaries between man and God.

zealous, destroying much that was of value in conveying the Christian message.

The only enduring Christian symbols that are universally recognised and widely used are the cross and the fish.[36] Early Christians probably did not use the cross, even though today it is the best-known Christian symbol, being present in, or outside, practically every church building. In the first Century, the cross was probably used by enemies of the Gospel who daubed the sign as a token of abuse on the homes of Christians in much the same way the Nazis painted the 'Star of David' on the front of Jewish homes before and during the Second World War. The cross only became widely adopted as a Christian symbol in the 4th Century after Constantine, alerted by a remarkable visionary experience, used the cross as an ensign in his victorious military campaign to become the undisputed emperor of the Roman Empire.

The cross is undoubtedly the most powerful of Christian symbols, but even this may speak different messages in different contexts and to different people. The sanitised polished wood cross that decorates so many churches is a far cry from the harsh reality of the shame and suffering of the cross at Calvary. Furthermore, although for the Christian today the cross is a symbol of God's sacrificial love, for the follower of Islam that same cross is a symbol of war, of persecution and genocide, emblazoned as it was on the shields of the Crusaders who massacred the inhabitants of Jerusalem – Jew, Christian and Moslem alike – when that city was recaptured in the first Crusade. Consequently, in Islamic countries, Christians need to be very sensitive about the public display of the cross.

Leading Worship

Acoustics and visual aspects

---

[36] The 'fish' is the oldest symbol of Christianity, dating from the first Century. Its use derives from the Greek word for fish *icthus* that forms an acrostic in Greek with the meaning: Jesus Christ, Son of God, Saviour. The symbol, a fish in outline, is most usually encountered today away from the church building as car stickers or in logos of Christian businesses and so on.

Place

As a leader you may or may not have much control over the place of worship, but it is important to realise that the worship environment has an important influence on the preparation and conduct of worship. Both acoustic and visual considerations are crucial as well as an awareness of potential distractions and hazards. In this latter category are ceiling fans which blow away leading notes or OHP transparencies and howling babies who render 'times of silence' a misnomer. The art of worship leading involves making the best use of the resources to hand and this includes the place of worship.

Key questions to be asked include: i) Can you be heard adequately by the congregation? ii) Can you and your visual aids, whether Communion elements or OHP slides, be clearly seen? Obviously the extent of the problem depends on the venue, whether a church building, open air, or a room in someone's home, but the questions remain the same. If you are not familiar with the meeting place, you would be well advised to arrive early to check out the venue before the worship, at the same time making sure you have advised your contact person in respect of any special requirements. Remember, hearing and sight are a function not only of the building but also the congregation. Since sight and hearing begin to deteriorate from the mid-twenties, greater consideration must be given as the average age of the congregation increases.

In church buildings, many pulpits and lecterns are equipped with microphones, but at various points in the service, *e.g.*, receiving the offertory or conducting a baptism, you may not be amplified, and it will be necessary for you to project your voice so as to be heard adequately. Beware! The microphone may well be on all the time and may pick up whispered asides to assistants, or the leader's croak during times of singing. If you do not have a good singing voice, then it is wise to step back from the mike or use considerably reduced volume to avoid distracting the congregation.

Using the Overhead Projector

If you are planning to use visual aids, make sure they can be seen from the back of the building. Ensure that the OHP screen is visible[37] to the congregation but out of direct sunlight. If a screen is not available, a light coloured wall or a white bed sheet can be reasonably adequate substitutes. If using the OHP in daylight conditions, use dark colours: black, blue, brown, and not lighter colours such as: yellow, orange or red which are much less visible. Remember to prepare transparencies with adequately sized letters.[38]

Where possible, have a dedicated operator for the OHP as it is usually not feasible for the leader to also show the transparencies whilst leading the worship. The transparencies, in correct order, should be provided to the operator before the service, together with a copy of the order of service indicating when the slides are to be displayed. When showing song lyrics, it is helpful if the operator displays only the relevant verse and covers the remainder of the slide. The words can be progressively displayed as the hymn is sung. But remember, people read more rapidly than they sing so it is helpful always to display at least one line beyond the line that is being sung. If possible, avoid having the words of one song on several transparencies as it is a tricky operation to slickly substitute slides in mid-song.

Make full use of the OHP as it is a versatile but simple to operate piece of equipment. It can helpfully be used to display pictures, or words of welcome, or to summarise important notices or information. It can also be used creatively in illustrating children's talks or adult sermons. If there is an artist or cartoonist in the congregation, their gifts can be fully utilised. The OHP can also be used for shadow plays – either in

---

[37] Don't forget the congregation will need to see over the heads of the people in front when standing to sing.

[38] Normally a font size of 26pt is adequate for full screen projection. For best effect use **bold** print and lowercase letters. Capital letters are harder to read, especially for children, and do not allow one to distinguish proper names. For example, GOD could be read as either God or god, FATHER as Father or father. The computer output can be printed directly onto a special transparency or photocopied onto a transparency. But do **not** use ordinary transparencies for hand writing in a photocopier as they may melt in the machine!

conventional mode or back projecting onto a white sheet. The possibilities are almost endless.

It is very helpful if there is someone responsible for the maintenance of the equipment. The OHP needs routine cleaning, as the various lenses both inside and outside the box are magnets for dust.[39] If the projector is extensively used it is advisable to purchase a two-bulb model. This allows instant changeover to the spare bulb should the first bulb blow during use. However, as worship leader, always be prepared for the worst-case scenario – the power cut. The worship should not completely collapse if there is no electricity. Prepare and plan accordingly.

Multi-media equipment

Many prosperous town or city churches have already moved beyond the OHP age and have installed a variety of equipment networked in with a fixed LCD projector, usually mounted on the ceiling of the worship centre. This can be interfaced with video cameras, VCR, VCD, computers, digitised OHP *etc*. These can be used to provide song lyrics, computer graphics, video clips and so on. A full discussion of the possibilities is beyond the scope of this book and the experience of the author but some general information can be found elsewhere.[40] Many churches will have some whiz kid – probably a teenager – who can provide useful insight as to the possibilities and maybe the enthusiasm to make them happen.

PA Systems and amplification

Probably one of the most disruptive elements of contemporary worship is the use of PA systems. Whereas the amplification of voices or music used in a creative and sensitive way can greatly benefit worship, the abuse of amplification, especially excessive volume levels, can greatly disrupt worship. The amplifiers and microphones should be adjusted

---

[39] The light output from the projector is greatly reduced if the various lenses are dirty.
[40] Draper (2000) 36-44

and tested[41] before the worship begins and further adjustments made as necessary during the course of worship. Preferably the amplifier controls should be at the rear of the building or in a console in the centre of the auditorium so that the technician can hear the sound as it is for the congregation and not the people on stage.

It is helpful if feedback can be routinely obtained from the congregation to ensure that the volume levels are adequate but not excessive. In general, modern music (keyboard, guitars and drums) tends to be played too loudly to sensitively accompany and encourage corporate singing. The same is often true of the worship leader or lead singer. The aim should always be to lead and accompany, not to perform, or overpower the congregation.

Seating Arrangements

Acoustic and visual problems are frequently compounded by the congregation, who, in a mostly empty building, insist on sitting in the rear few pews. This is a crucial but potentially explosive issue. Some church members are so wedded to their particular seat that one would be excused for thinking that pew rentals had never been abolished! This phenomenon can have a disastrous effect on worship since, not only are seeing and hearing handicapped, but fellowship is disrupted and the singing is crippled. Ideally, the seating of the congregation needs to be compact and the building size appropriate to the group for meaningful corporate worship. Thus a fellowship group of say eight persons might worship effectively in a small room, but the same number arranged randomly around a building with a seating capacity of five hundred would be a disaster for *living worship*.

There are a number of ways of tackling this problem but all require sensitivity. The solutions will also depend on whether you are a regular member of the congregation concerned, and so know the problem in advance, or whether you are a guest of the church. The most radical solution is to meet in a more appropriately sized place, *e.g.*, the vestry

---

[41] Microphones should be tested by voice and not by tapping the microphone as this can cause damage to this sensitive instrument.

Place 153

rather than the sanctuary.[42] Alternatively, rear pews may be roped off or chairs stacked to limit the places where people are free to sit. But beware! People can become very upset and angry at these tactics, as to disturb their seating may give rise to a sense of insecurity.[43] The back row is after all sufficiently insulated from all but the most vigorous of preachers, and to move forward must put the worshipper in jeopardy of actually hearing a sermon![44]

If you have no control over where people sit before the service begins, there are still two possible avenues of approach. The first is the Billy Graham type of solution that asks people to get up out of their seats and to come down to the front. This approach should only be used where you are reasonably confident of response. If people are too embarrassed to move or too outraged to think of leaving 'their' seats, then you have lost control of the service even before it has begun and the worship atmosphere will be spoilt.

The Billy Graham solution requires a blend of sensitivity, reasonableness and opportunity. Firstly, you must understand how the people feel, being especially aware of any who may be sitting at the back for special reasons, such as nursing a baby or being newcomers. Secondly, it is often helpful to explain to the group why you are asking them to move. For example, you could explain that coming nearer the front and closer together would symbolise drawing nearer to God and to one another as members of the Family of God. Thirdly, you need to provide a reasonable opportunity for movement to take place with the minimum amount of embarrassment or disturbance. This might be

---

[42] This has the added advantage of saving on heating bills in cold European winters.

[43] On one occasion I was preaching and leading a service with the theme 'Coping with change'. In order to illustrate this I rearranged the seating in the worship centre. Instead of regular straight rows of seats facing the front wall of the building I substituted a series of curves focussing on the centre at the front. Some of the regular worshippers were highly indignant because they were unable to find 'their' seat. Their feelings were addressed in the message which tackled the whole question of how, as Christians, we should deal with change and the unknown

[44] Ironically, as all teachers will know, it is actually those who sit at the back that are most visible to the preacher/ leader and often the most distracting!

accomplished by using the opening hymn as a processional, and asking the people to move as it is sung. The movement can be catalysed by people you have asked in advance to make the first move.

A simpler solution, at least for the congregation, is for you to leave the pulpit or lectern and move down among the congregation. If they will not come to join you at the front you can join them at the rear. This is not particularly easy for the inexperienced. There is no pulpit to hide behind or lectern to steady shaking hands, and there is need for either fewer books or a clever arrangement of the same. Nevertheless, when well done, it is less confrontational for the congregation and yet changes the whole dynamic of the worship and can make a lasting impression.

Seating is very important. It is a kind of body language. If we sit apart from our fellow worshippers we are saying we are separate from them, we do not belong together, we consider our worship from an individualistic point of view. As we sit together, so we learn to worship together and begin to realise that we are indeed part of the Body of Christ, and that we can encourage one another in worship. Sitting together also transforms the singing that is such an important part of our worship.

Where the congregation are seated on chairs rather than fixed pews this opens up possibilities of alternative seating arrangements. Sitting in a circle around the Lord's Table can be a moving setting for a Holy Communion service, whereas a curve or semicircle can be a refreshing change from straight lines, making it easier for congregational participation and increasing the sense of oneness. Even here, one must exercise a certain caution, as any change can disturb the sensibilities of the ardent churchgoer who has perhaps yet to learn that their security lies in Christ and not the seating arrangement!

Summary

In this chapter we have re-emphasised the biblical teaching that the church building is to house the people of God rather than to serve as a temple for God. We have noted that the building has a profound

Place

influence on our worship and that its upkeep, décor and furnishings speak to us and touch our worship. Particularly influential are the size and comfort of the worship centre and where people sit. The worship leader must make every effort to ensure that the worship centre is properly prepared, and the facilities properly used to enhance the worship. Advanced preparation and teamwork are the key.

9 – Preparation

Appropriate preparation is vital in the search for *living worship*. Preparation is multi-faceted and includes preparing: oneself, the order of service, the worship team, the congregation and the place of worship. All these are essential, although not all may be under the direct control of the leader. In this chapter we shall look together at the first three aspects detailed above.

Preparation of Self

In a sense, as we have discussed earlier, the whole of life is a preparation for leading worship – as it is for preaching, or indeed sharing our faith. Yet, at the same time, the act of leading worship focuses our attention on our personal walk with God in a fresh way. Whereas, technically, it is possible to produce a good order of worship and to present it clearly without attention to spiritual preparation, yet it is highly unlikely that the Spirit will work effectively through us under these circumstances, and the spiritual impact will be greatly diminished.

There are at least three aspects that need to be mentioned. Firstly, there is the need to deal with unconfessed sin, which affects our relationship with God and with our brothers and sisters in Christ. There may be a necessity to say sorry to others, or to make amends, as clearly taught by Jesus.[1] Secondly, there is a need to develop a daily 'walk' with God, or, as many would describe it today, to be 'led by the Spirit'. Through such a 'walk' one becomes increasingly conscious of His presence in daily life situations, and consequently in public worship too. This is greatly aided by a regular system of Bible reading, by time set aside for prayer and worship, by involvement in Christian fellowship, and by service.

---

[1] Mat 5:23,24

Thirdly, it may be helpful to use some spiritual exercise in preparation for leading worship. The simplest is perhaps prayer focused on the preparation of the service, the actual worship and the congregation who will be present. Some find it helpful to fast – perhaps to go without breakfast if it is a morning service or without a later meal if the worship is in the evening. These are reminders that we are involved in something special and enable us to seek the Lord's power and strength. In addition, from a practical perspective, it is not helpful to lead or preach after a heavy meal.

Preparation of the Service

Preliminary

The first thing to emphasise is to start early – probably at least two weeks before the actual date. Begin by finding out the full details of the service and exactly what you are required to do. Part of the checklist will include:

- How much (what part) of the service am I leading?
- Who else is leading/ preaching? Is there an organist/ pianist or a music team? How and when can I contact them?
- What is the occasion or theme of the service? (*E.g.*, Easter, Lent, Harvest, anniversary celebration.)
- What is special about the service? (*E.g.*, Family service, Communion, Healing service and so on.)
- Who will be there? (*E.g.*, Age groups, children, and approximate numbers.)
- What are the lectionary readings? (If used by the church.)
- What is the specific theme of the sermon and what special requirements (if any) does the preacher have?
  (*E.g.*, Scripture reading, hymns, positioning of the sermon, visual aid equipment.)
- Do other people normally assist with the worship?
  (*E.g.*, Musicians, choir, scripture readers, intercessors)
- What facilities are available? (PA system, OHP, LCD projector, white-boards *etc.*)

Preparation 157

- What hymnbooks or songbooks are normally used and are available? Can words of other songs be printed on a notice sheet or displayed with an OHP, or LCD projector?
- Are there any special worship traditions or arrangements? (*E.g.*, Offerings received at the door, children leaving midway through the service, notices given by...)
- What is the normal order[2] and length of the service?

Of course things are much easier if you lead worship in your own church because you will already know the answers to many of the above questions. Whereas it is usually appropriate to follow most of the local church traditions, these are not sacrosanct. For example, you might like to suggest that it is more appropriate for a local church leader to give out the announcements, or to request assistance in reading Scripture passages or in leading prayer. However, do not put people on the spot! Ask in advance, don't be disappointed by refusal and be prepared to be let down.[3]

Tentative Outline

Using the information you have obtained, begin to work on the order of service, perhaps using a structure such as discussed in Chapter 3. Prepare an outline.[4] This outline will include essential ingredients such as: hymns/ songs/ choruses, prayers, children's talk (if appropriate), scripture readings, offering, sermon and any other items such as testimonies, dance, choir, drama and the like. The opportunities for prayer will cover such aspects as: our approach to God, confession, praise, thanksgiving, intercession and some kind of closing prayer of dedication or blessing.[5] Make sure that the draft order provides a

---

[2] This may be defined by a prepared liturgy or the custom of the church. Even non-liturgical churches have their own unwritten liturgy or normal order for worship.

[3] For example, on one occasion, a church where I was leading worship had agreed to provide someone to lead prayers of intercession. On arrival at the church, the person who had apparently been asked, curtly refused.

[4] Use pencil and paper or computer – work with whatever you are comfortable.

[5] Suggestions for leading prayer in corporate worship have already been discussed in detail in Chapter 4.

suitable opportunity for children to leave or enter (if necessary), for an offering to be taken up and for notices to be given out.

Draft Outline

The tentative worship outline may look something like the following[6]:

Call to Worship
[Prayer/ Scripture verse/Chorus]

Opening Hymn

Prayer of confession

Assurance of forgiveness
[Verse of Scripture[7]]

The Lord's Prayer

Praise and Thanksgiving
[Hymn/ Choruses/ Open prayer/ Praise Response/Dance]

The Offering
[Hymn/silence/music]

Dedication of the Offering
[Prayer/Chorus/Scripture]

Testimony[8]

Scripture Reading(s)
[Maybe preceded by hymn or chorus]

Hymn of Preparation
[Relating to the theme or a longing for God to speak]

The Message

Response/Fellowship Time
[Song/Hymn/Greetings/Prayer/Ministry]

Prayers of Intercession

Closing Hymn

Final Prayer

Notices

---

[6] Obviously many different outlines can be used; this is but one example.

[7] For example Ps 32:1,5; 51:2,9; 65:3; 79:9; 85:2; 103:10,12 or 1 John 1:8,9

[8] This might equally be included in the time of praise and thanksgiving.

Preparation 159

Of course the actual outline may be determined by a set liturgy and this then will be your starting point. Whereas it may not be permissible to omit items from the liturgy, it is nearly always possible to interpret and enrich the liturgy with appropriate introductions, hymns, prayers *etc.* As far as possible avoid working outside of the liturgy. For example, resist the temptation to add a block of praise songs before the liturgy, as there should be a point where praise naturally occurs within the liturgy.

There are several good reasons for avoiding the creation of a praise time before the liturgy. Firstly, it puts praise in the wrong place ahead of confession. Before we are right with God through confession and forgiveness we are not ready to freely praise God.[9] Secondly, it diminishes the role of the liturgical worship since it implies that the liturgy cannot accommodate praise in a modern idiom. Thirdly, it allows traditionalists to avoid this additional emphasis on praise by arriving late, just in time for the liturgy, or what they consider to be the 'proper worship'.

Choosing Hymns, Songs and Choruses

Having drafted an outline, then proceed to shortlist suitable hymns, songs or choruses. In order to make appropriate choices you need to be aware of:

➢ The resources – what hymnbooks/ songbooks or facilities for providing words (OHP/ Notice sheet) are available.

➢ The nature of the congregation and their worship experience, that is, whether there are children or teenagers present and what hymns are well known or familiar.

➢ The theme of the service, the church calendar, the aim of the sermon. (These have been discussed earlier in Chapter 5).

➢ The order and flow of the service.[10]

---

[9] See for example King David's longing for forgiveness so that he could again praise God (Psalm 51).

[10] Hymns at the beginning or end of a service, during the offering or before a reading or message will all be quite distinct.

For example, an opening hymn should help the congregation to focus on the presence of God and enable them to draw near to Him. Bear in mind the nature and worship experience of the congregation, especially whether there are children or young people present.[11]

In choosing hymns or songs you need to make full use of the resources and occasionally introduce something new if particularly appropriate to the theme. The selection must be tailored to both the service and the congregation. This means that the choice of hymns will vary from church to church even with the same overall theme and may even be different for a morning and evening congregation. Aim at balance and variety.[12]

Balance means that you will always have some hymns/ choruses that are very familiar to the congregation so as to permit evocative association. (Don't forget the children, who also have worship memories even if they are shorter!) It is always helpful to begin and end with something well known so as to start and end the service on a positive note. This means that you should avoid completely new or obscure hymns at the start or conclusion of the service. Balance also means that you will be unafraid to use choruses, where it is appropriate to do so, even in the most traditional congregations, and that you will seek to vary the nature of the hymns in terms of meter, length, tune *etc.*

Having made appropriate choices, add your hymns, songs or choruses to your draft outline – include alternatives if there appear to be more than one that is appropriate. Check, if necessary, with the musician or preacher, the suitability of the choices. Finalise the choice.

---

[11] One should also choose carefully at services such as weddings, funerals, and evangelistic rallies where there may be a high proportion of people who rarely attend a worship service. Not only should one choose well-known hymns or songs, but also avoid lyrics which use a lot of religious metaphors or 'in language', such as references to worshipping 'the Lamb that was slain'.

[12] Some of the aspects of balance have been discussed in Ch 7. There needs to be enough corporate emphasis in the lyrics, and the songs should cover several aspects of worship, not just praise. It is good to have a balance musically as well.

Preparation

Overview of the Service

At this stage, using the draft outline, 'picture' your way through the whole service, 'seeing' what the congregation and the leader will be doing. Ensure that there is a balance of congregational participation and movement (sitting, standing *etc*) and envisage where and how the children will leave. Check that the placing of the offering fits in with the custom of the church.[13] Think about the mechanics of the offering, whether it easier for the congregation to get their gifts ready whilst seated or standing. If using a hymn during the offering, try to think whether the offering can be completed before the hymn ends. If not, what is to happen? Do you want to repeat a verse, or to remain standing whilst the music continues to be played?

If it is a baptism or communion service you need to think about where the baptismal party will sit for easy access to the front and whether or not the baptismal candidates are going to give a brief testimony. For a communion service you also need to think about how the bread and wine are going to be distributed and the mechanics of the congregation coming to the communion rail or being served in their seats.

Informing Others

Write, or preferably type out, a finalised order of worship that should then be made available to the organist, musicians and others who are taking part in the service. Ensure this is at least two or three days before the service so that the musicians can adequately prepare. Instruct lesson readers as to what point to come to the front to read and as to whether they will come up unannounced. Consider writing short introductions to the Scripture readings.

Provide the OHP operator with all the required transparencies in the correct order as well as a complete order of service with all the songs clearly marked. You might like to highlight with a colour pen the songs that involve the use of the OHP.

---

[13] In some churches the children may act as stewards to take up the offering, but this is rather difficult if you have just sent them to their Sunday School class!

Preparing prayers and introductions

Prepare the prayers that you are going to use. Even if you always pray extempore prayers, make a note of the direction or substance of the prayer to avoid repetition or divergence. This has been discussed in some detail in Chapter 4 on prayer. If it is prayer associated with a sacramental service such as baptism or the Lord's Supper, ensure that you carefully think through the theology of your prayer if you are not using a liturgy or set prayer. Make sure what you pray is biblical and sound, otherwise you may confuse the congregation.

Work out and write down the link phrases that you are going to use to introduce or join together each part of the service. You may not actually need to refer to the script, but it pays dividends to plan in advance, and if your mind suddenly goes blank, you have something to fall back on. In particular, think how you are going to begin the service, in a way that lets people know that their business is worship and their focus God.

Decide which parts of the service can flow or link together without comment. For example, sometimes several songs might flow together without connecting introductions, although often brief comments can be very helpful to focus the people's thoughts on the meaning of the song or how it is being used in the worship.[14] In some cases it may not be necessary to announce the Scripture readings if the reader can follow the order of service and be in place to read at the appropriate time.

Introduction of a visiting preacher should be kept brief and to the point – a word of welcome, his or her name and perhaps occupation or place of origin and the theme of the message. It is not necessary to give a complete biography!

The Written Service

One of the key decisions to be made is how to summarise the overall order of service. Different people use a variety of systems. The important thing is to have one that works for *you*. This may necessitate

---

[14] For example, you might wish to say that the congregation is going to sing the song as: 'a prayer', or as 'an act of thanksgiving', or as 'the offering is taken up', or as 'an act of personal dedication' and so on.

Preparation 163

trying out different schemes and eventually evolving your own way of doing things. The system that you use will depend on your circumstances and the facilities that are available to you.

In devising your own system you need to bear in mind the following:

> Aim for simplicity – avoid having numerous books, papers and prompts.

> Have materials that are clearly legible under pulpit conditions. (*Poor lighting/ non-optimum reading distance/ stress.*)

> Ensure that you have a summary of the *whole* service including all hymn numbers – you may not be in a position to see the hymn board or you may forget which number is next.

> Have a system that allows you to file material for future reference or use.[15]

A Practical System

Over the years I have come around to using the following system that has a number of advantages, especially if leading the whole service. The overall order of service is typed out, suitably spaced, on an A5 size sheet.[16] The use of a Word Processor, if available, makes the task much easier.[17] (Of course it could equally be handwritten on lined paper.)

The order of service is headed with the date, occasion, church and time of service (carefully checked).[18] The whole order is then summarised with all the ingredients of the worship clearly shown, including hymn numbers and first lines of hymns. A copy of this order of service is then

---

[15] There is no need for you to reinvent the wheel or start from the beginning each time you lead a service.

[16] This is half the size of an A4 sheet – and is approximately the page size of this book.

[17] When using a Word Processor, save the files for future reference. You may be able to use the same service structure and simply change the ingredients. It may be advisable to print the main details in quite large print sizes, e.g., font 16pt, so as to be easily visible under all circumstances.

[18] This information will ensure that you avoid repeating the same service if invited again to the same church.

made available to the musicians and other participants. The copy is marked to denote their responsibility.

Hymn numbers are highlighted with a marker pen for easy reading. Different colours can be used to denote different hymn/ songbooks or the use of the OHP or LCD projector. If the words of the hymn are being projected on the screen, it is best for the leader to have a copy of the words so that there is no need to turn to face the screen.

Introductory phrases are written in on my copy usually a few hours before the service so that they are still fresh in the mind. Prayers for different parts of the service are typed or hand written on separate A5 sheets. Prayers from books can be copied out, photocopied and pasted, or scanned and printed onto the A5 paper.[19]

The loose A5 sheets containing the order of service, hymn words (if necessary) and prayers are then arranged into a small folder of A5 size plastic pages in the order in which they will appear in the service. The small file is easily hand-held and can be used in or out of the pulpit.

On The Day

Arrive early! Half an hour before the service is ideal, especially if there are any last minute arrangements to be done.[20] This also allows a margin of safety in case you miss the bus, have a puncture or the car fails to start. Arriving early will not prevent things going wrong but it will at least give you time to do something about it. Any extra time is a bonus that can be used for prayer. Check as much of the detail as possible, especially any particular requirements such as the use of songbooks, participation of readers, inclusion of song lyrics in the notice sheet *etc*. Remember: it may be the usher's job to hand out the correct books but it will be your problem if a mistake has been made!

---

[19] It is advantageous to put prayers on separate sheets as these can then be filed separately later on. In this way you can build up a collection of prayers or prayer outlines suitable for: confession, praise, thanksgiving, intercession and so on.

[20] For example, setting up the OHP or screen.

Preparation

The Leading Place

Depending on the worship centre, you may be leading the service from a pulpit, lectern or music stand! Prepare the leading place early before the congregation start to arrive. Check the heights of adjustable stands, and the positioning and operation of microphones.[21] Remove all books, old notices *etc*, except the ones you need to use. Check you have all that is required: hymnbook, songbook, Bible, liturgy *etc*. Place an order of service central on the stand[22] in addition to the order in your hand-held file. Open and mark the places in the hymnbook, at least the opening hymn; mark the place for scripture readings.[23] Have your book of prayers/ notes open and to hand.

Prior preparation means that the beginning of the service is not marred by a hiatus while the congregation waits for the worship leader to finish arranging his or her materials. Have a look around the church from the leading place. Get the feel of the atmosphere. Note where people are sitting. Ascertain whether you have a chair to sit on. Mentally plot your course from the leading point to the front to receive the offering and note where the offering should most appropriately be placed and how to get it there!

The Musicians

You may be working with one person such as an organist, or pianist or a team of musicians. You will have contacted these people earlier and preferably provided them with a complete order of service. Try to have a final check with the music team and ensure that they have a copy of the complete order of service – not just the numbers or titles of hymns[24]

---

[21] Make sure the microphone is on and the volume adjusted appropriately – unless of course there is a technician who adjusts the volume during the course of the service.

[22] If you place the order of service in a transparent plastic sleeve it makes it easier to handle and less likely to be blown away by draughts or ceiling fans.

[23] If using a hymnbook it is actually a good idea to provide a numbered bookmark for each hymn (1, 2, 3, *etc*) or use *Post-it* stickers to mark the pages with actual hymn numbers.

[24] As a precaution against making a mistake it is helpful to provide both the song number and its title or first line.

– and are aware of any special requirements. Be as helpful as you can to the organist/ musicians as their contribution can make or ruin a worship service. Be willing to accept their advice as they may well know the musical capabilities of the congregation best.

Prayer Room or Vestry

As early as possible try to retire to a quiet place: the vestry, church office, or prayer room for a time of quiet and prayer. Pray for the congregation while they are arriving, for the service and for yourself. Sometimes there will be a prayer meeting before the service that you may like to join, or normally one of the church leaders, deacons or stewards will pray with you before the worship begins.

Double check whether there are any major events, serious illnesses or deaths within the congregation of which you need to be aware. Be prepared to include any last minute but important issues in your prayers. Try to avoid getting involved in general conversation which distracts from your preparation – there will be opportunity for that after the service. Surrender the service into God's hands.

Summary

Worship leading is a vital ministry in the life of the church and requires adequate preparation. The areas specifically focussed in this chapter include: the leader's personal spiritual life, the preparation of the order of worship, and the practical arrangements in the worship centre on the day. All are vitally important.

10 – Presentation

Having just looked at the task of preparation for leading worship, we now move on to think through the issue of presentation. In particular, we are going to deal with the crucial issue of how to link the ingredients of worship together into a meaningful whole, especially, what to say and what not to say! As we do this, we need to be reminded that we are aiming for holistic worship. Consequently, the contents and presentation of our worship needs to be designed to incorporate: the whole person – heart, soul, mind and strength; and involve the participation of the whole congregation.

In the third chapter we reflected that worship should have direction and should flow smoothly to a climax. Whereas the correct choice of appropriate ingredients is important, the actual presentation and the words used to link the parts together are vital. The link phrases are also important in drawing attention to, explaining and emphasising the overall theme of worship.

The Language of Worship Leading

Every Word is Precious

In daily life we use words so carelessly and mindlessly that we need to relearn how to use words when it comes to leading worship. The first thing that we need to realise as we approach worship is that: every word is precious! On reflection we might be more Christ-like if we observed this rule in our daily lives.

Many of the words used in worship are fixed; for example, the lyrics of hymns or psalms, or the wording of set prayers or readings, or the text of the liturgy. For this part of the worship our only freedom is limited to the choice of the initial material.[1] However, there are very significant parts of the worship where we have complete control over the words, for example, our own prayer compositions, whether extempore or pre-written, and crucially the link phrases that join together different parts of the service. It is on this latter aspect that we shall concentrate here.

As in life, so in worship, words may be: helpful or hindering, essential or irrelevant, truthful or deceitful, self-centred or inclusive, informative or confusing, encouraging or destroying, loving or hurtful, challenging or compromising, beautiful or coarse, uplifting or depressing. The challenge for the worship leader is to make the right use of words. In a way this is a natural development of the emphasis on *whole life* worship. Our daily lives need to embrace this challenge so that our worship leading is a natural outcome of our daily conversations. For it to be otherwise, is for our worship leading to be *play-acting*, or, as Jesus put it, hypocrisy.[2]

The preciousness of words is felt even more keenly in leading worship because of time limitations. Unnecessary speech reduces the time available for that which is pure gold; for example, to spend time drawing attention to routine announcements, already available on printed sheets, is anathema to good worship leading. Not only is it time wasting, but it also distracts and dilutes the things that are central to worship. We must therefore concern ourselves both with what we say, and what we need not, or should not, say.

The Purpose of Words

Before examining some specific examples it is helpful to reflect on the actual purpose of words. Fundamentally, words enable communication. Of course, we must never forget they are not the sole means of communication, nor necessarily, even the most effective. For example, on one occasion, my wife had been reminding me for several weeks

---

[1] For example, we may have a choice in the version of the Bible used for the Scripture reading, although usually it is more helpful to read the version that is used by the majority of members.

[2] The word hypocrisy comes from the Greek word, *hupokrites*, which is used to translate Jesus' criticism of the Pharisees, and is the word used for an actor in the Greek drama.

Presentation

that I had promised to hang some pictures but without success. Finally, in desperation to communicate the urgency of the request, she placed my hammer and the picture hooks on my desk, on top of my sermon preparation! Needless to say the symbolic message was received loud and clear and the pictures were soon hung.

Apart from symbolism, body language is also a powerful means of getting across ideas and feelings. Body language involves all that we communicate by our physical presence. Our eyes and facial expressions speak volumes, so do our posture and our gestures. Usually, our body language is more open and honest than our words and this is why a trained counsellor will listen not only to the words of her client but also the unconscious messages that are transmitted. As worship leaders we need to be so genuine that our bodies speak the same message as our words; moreover, that our eyes show Christ's love and our faces radiate with the joy of worship and adoration.

What is it that needs to be communicated in worship? Firstly, there is the overall ethos or atmosphere of worship. That aspect which makes the stranger in the midst feel welcome, the regular members aware that they are part of a real fellowship, and all cognizant of the fact that we have come to worship and encounter the Living God. Words that open our eyes to the understanding that worship is more than a social gathering of friends; it is a uniting together to acknowledge that Christ is the Lord of our lives. Words that help to bring worship alive, to affirm that worship is inextricably bound up with our daily living, that God is not remote and distant but near at hand, willing to touch and be touched. Words that encourage and uplift and draw people into his presence, to offer Him the praise that is His due.

Secondly, words provide information. On a basic level, the leader's words are like stage directions, or the conductor's baton, enabling the congregation and other participants, such as musicians and readers, to know what to do, when and how to do it. To be able to give clear instructions, which people can follow without difficulty, is a prerequisite for effective corporate worship. There is nothing more embarrassing as a worshipper, than not being sure what one is expected to do, especially if you are a stranger, or are sitting on the front row. It is always crucial that people know whether they are expected to sit or stand, or what to do with communion elements, and when they are going to be confronted with an offering bag! Similarly, the congregation must be informed of the hymn number or the page of the service book and so on.

Thirdly, words are enlightening. They provide understanding, explain why things are being done and point to the significance of various aspects of the worship. Thus the leader may draw attention to the theme of the service, or the special significance of a hymn, or the background of a scripture reading. Similarly, it would be appropriate to draw attention to any special cause for which the offering is to be used, or perhaps to make people aware of a recent death, before the bereaved family are prayed for. Such a use of words helps the worship to be meaningful.

Lastly, words, and the way in which they are spoken, will determine the relationship that the leader has with the people, and the people with each other and God. There is a very real tension here. On the one hand, the leader really needs to be in the background so that the worship reflects the glory of God and not the adulation of the leader; on the other hand, the leader needs to have sufficient *presence*, or authority, so that instructions are followed and the service can proceed in an orderly manner.[3] Again the leader needs to be sufficiently *one* with the people so that there is a real sense of corporateness, yet not so chummy and relaxed that there is a sense of irreverence.

What to Say

Some readers may object to this and the following section since they may appear too prescriptive and sometimes judgemental. My defence is that it is probably best to give some actual examples rather than vague generalisations so that the reader will know what is being talked about. However, it needs to be recognised that there are no easy answers to these questions. What we say will depend, to some extent, on our own personality, vocabulary and Christian experience, and also on that of

---

[3] By authority we are not referring to a headmaster or sergeant major style whereby the congregation are ordered to comply. Leadership needs to be clear, convincing and encouraging so that the people readily follow the leader's instructions.

our congregation. For example, the words used for a Sunday School class will be different from those appropriate to an adult congregation. We need to be genuine and natural, and yet our words need to be informed by some of the considerations we have already looked at. Learning to lead worship is inevitably a constant learning experience that will be slowly but surely transformed by our increasing expertise, as well as our growth in Christian holiness.

Introductions

Perhaps the place to start is with introductions, for example, announcing a hymn. The first thing to consider is what does the congregation already know. Is it necessary to repeat this information? Are there other things which people need to know? For example:

- The number of the hymn and which book it is in.
- Whether to sit, stand or do something else while singing.
- Any special instructions about singing the hymn, omitting verses, singing in parts, singing as a prayer *etc*.
- Information about the hymn – its authorship, tune, significance, relation to theme or the point in the service.
- Any special events that will take place in the service during the singing of the hymn.[4]

As the reader will see, there is a wealth of potential information to be given and it is most important to distinguish between that which is essential, that which is helpful, that which is unnecessary, and as we shall see later, that which is positively distracting. Much of this depends on what the congregation already knows.

Let's look at the above information in more detail – firstly, the hymn number or book. Almost every church or fellowship group is different and has its own tradition and the reader needs to work out carefully what information needs to be given. However, always make allowance for the newcomer who may not be aware of the system. If an OHP is used to screen the words, possibly only the musicians need to know the

---

[4] For example, taking up of the offering, Sunday School children to leave *etc*.

number of the hymn, unless of course there are congregational members who have poor eyesight and prefer to follow in a book. (The number and book reference can helpfully be included on the OHP slide.)

In some churches, a complete printed order is given at the beginning of the service that includes hymn numbers. If this is the case it is strictly not necessary to repeat the numbers, providing the congregation are aware of the system. On occasions, it may then be appropriate for the musicians simply to play a few introductory bars without any formal introduction. If the congregation are dependent on oral information, then give the number clearly, and after any other introduction, repeat the number once more. If more than one book is used, the congregation will often follow visual signs if the leader holds up the book for the people to see. If you are leading worship in a different church, make sure you know how to refer to the book according to local custom.[5]

Churches often have traditions as to the appropriate posture for singing hymns. Most congregations stand to sing hymns, but not always. In charismatic worship it is usually the norm to stand to sing praise choruses. In many cases it may not be necessary to give instructions to sit or stand providing that you are following the normal pattern of the church concerned. However, whenever there is doubt, give clear instruction. This is especially important where you are changing a customary practice; for example, you may feel it appropriate for the congregation to remain seated, or even to kneel, to sing a meditative or prayerful hymn. This should be clearly stated. The same is of course true at the end of the hymn. Some congregations are used to sitting immediately; others will remain standing until instructed to sit.

Special instructions about singing hymns should also be given clearly. If the congregation is to sing in parts, it may be necessary for continued leading during the course of singing. On the whole, avoid omitting verses unless pre-planned and there is a very good reason for doing so. Often when services have run over time the leader is tempted to shorten the final hymn. To omit a one-minute verse when the service is 45

---

[5] For example, the book may be variously referred to as the: hymnbook, songbook, chorus book, worship book, hymn supplement, blue book *etc.*

Presentation

minutes too long is an act of tokenism. Inevitably this is done on the spur of the moment, usually the wrong verse or verses are left out and the service ends on a note of confusion with everyone singing different words. The potential for shortening the worship should be planned into the service and not left as an afterthought.

Sometimes it may be helpful to give the background to the writing of a hymn if it adds to an understanding of the hymn, but beware of interesting but unnecessary comments on the hymn-writer or tune. On one occasion I attended a service where each of the 5 hymns was accompanied by a 2-3 minute potted history. It was very interesting, but completely unconnected with the worship and very distracting. It is often very helpful to explain how the hymn fits into the theme or relates to the occasion or part of the service. It may be appropriate to focus on some of the key words from a verse, or to read a line from a verse.

How to say it?

Having first considered what needs to be said, the question still remains, how to say it? The answer must be: as simply and clearly as possible, but having said that, there is no one model. Two examples are given below to illustrate possible approaches. The first example is an introduction to the chorus entitled *Majesty*[6] that is to be used after a time of confession to lead into praise. A possible introduction could be as follows:

> As forgiven sinners let us respond to God in praise. We will sing chorus number three hundred and seventy-nine in the songbook.
>
> The chorus reminds us that Jesus is our king and worthy of our praise. *Majesty, worship His majesty, unto Jesus be glory, honour and praise.* (Quote of first two lines.)
>
> Number: three, five, eight.[7]
>
> Let us stand to sing![8]

---

[6] Songs of Fellowship (1991) 379.

[7] Only repeat if the number is not on a hymn-board or in the service sheet or you think some may not have heard it correctly the first time. It is helpful to say the words in a different format as some numbers can be confused, for example, thirteen and thirty. The first time it can be announced as 'thirty' and the second time as 'three-zero'.

Note, the number is best given early on in the introduction so that the worshippers can be finding the page whilst the remainder of the introduction is given.

The second example is an introduction for the children's hymn with the first line: *One more step along the world I go*. During the singing of the hymn the Sunday school children leave for their classes. The introduction might be given as follows:

> Hymn number seven hundred and forty-six: *One more step along the world I go*.
>
> The hymn likens the Christian life to a journey – a journey of discovery and sometimes discomfort. A journey in which we need to walk in step with our Lord.
>
> Hymn number: seven, four, six.
>
> The children will leave for their classes during the singing of the final verse.

In this case no instruction is given for the congregation to stand, as it is their normal practice to do so. Be careful to check up on how to refer to different groups within the church as they sometimes have special names. The children may be more appropriately referred to as: the Sunday School, or Sunday Club, or Young People, or Children's Church, or a bewildering array of other terms. Make sure you get it right!

Note, in both the suggestions above the words are *spoken* and not *read* and appropriate pauses are introduced to provide emphasis and to allow time for the worshipper to find the hymn numbers or to follow the instructions.

Noteworthy Phrases

Phrases need to be carefully used and chosen since, although they may appear to have the same meaning, there are differences in emphasis or

---

[8] Avoid informing the congregation that they are going to stand to sing the hymn at the beginning of the introduction otherwise there will be confusion. Inform the hymn number, allow time for the worshippers to find the page and only then invite everyone to stand to sing. Of course, it is different if the words are supplied on a screen.

nuance. For example, there are different ways of asking, requesting, or instructing people to stand during the service:

'Stand up!'	[*Authoritarian*]
'I would like you to stand...'	[*Self-centred/ tentative*]
'Will you please stand...?'	[*Tentative*]
'Please stand...'	[*Courteous*]
'Let us stand...'	[*Inclusive*]
'We will stand...'	[*Firm/Corporate*]

Similarly, when introducing prayer, leaders tend to use a range of phrases that include:

'Shall we pray...(?)'	[*Tentative*]
'Can we pray now...(?)'	[*Questioning capability*]
'May we pray.... (?)'	[*Seeking permission*]
'Let us pray...'	[*Inclusive*]
'We shall now pray...'	[*Firm/Corporate*]

Each of these phrases, although readily understood by most congregations, conveys a slightly different nuance as indicated in brackets above. In my view, instructions should not be tentative unless one is genuinely offering a choice. By far the best phrases are those that are inclusive, corporate and firm. These give the congregation a clear direction and yet do not set the leader apart.

Instructions or comments phrased in the form of questions invite an unwanted dialogue from the congregation. On one occasion I was present at a worship service where this actually happened. The leader had chosen a hymn with a tune that nobody knew and which didn't seem to fit the words. The leader didn't know the tune either and after five disastrous verses we all breathed a sigh of relief. But in order to salvage something from the shambles the leader couldn't resist commenting: "Well it's a beautiful tune, isn't it?" Audibly from the back row came a very firm reply: "No, it's not!" At that point I thought that the service was about to dissolve into a heated dialogue, but fortunately the leader merely spluttered in disbelief and continued with the service.

Coping with the unexpected

Worship really comes alive when the leader can ground the worship in the circumstances, sometimes unexpected, which surround and engulf the worship. This requires flexibility in conduct of the worship, the ability to think on one's feet, sensitivity to people and the Lord's leading, as well as the experience to know how to react to events which cannot be anticipated.

It may simply be drawing the congregation's attention to the beauty of the flowers on the Communion table that provide an insight into the beauty of God's creation. It may be the sun's rays that highlight the cross, or heavy rain that speaks to us of God's showers of blessing, or, strong winds that remind us of the Spirit's power and presence. Alternatively, it may be something that happens during the worship such as someone being taken suddenly ill. The leader responds by pausing to lead the congregation in prayer for the person while they are being attended to.

Then again a sudden power failure may threaten to wreck a well-planned service with all its dependence on modern electrical equipment.[9] However, a power failure, precisely because its effects are dramatic, could be used to provide a powerful spiritual lesson about the condition of Christians who are cut off from their power supply. After sharing this important truth, the people could be led to meditate and pray about their own condition.[10]

There are also painful and emotive experiences that inevitably affect the course of worship. A recent death of someone very close to the whole congregation, or a scandal involving church members or leaders, or perhaps a disaster in the local community, may well leave

---

[9] At one stroke one can easily find oneself without music (electronic keyboard), lyrics for the songs (OHP), lights and amplification system.

[10] The worship leader must not only use this opportunity but also make a rapid evaluation as to whether this is a temporary power-cut or is likely to last for the whole service. If the latter, it may require a radical reshaping of the worship, depending on how much the worship depends on electricity.

Presentation

people stunned.[11] The worship cannot continue as if nothing has happened if it is to be *living worship*. At the very minimum, a time of silence or prayer will be used to reflect and pray about the incidents.

Other happenings that might dramatically affect the course of a worship service are people coming under conviction of sin who need an opportunity for repentance, or those overwhelmed by an outpouring of the Holy Spirit. There is nothing in the planned service to deal with these situations, but the leader needs to stay calm and cope.[12]

There can also be more threatening interference. On one occasion I was present when a possessed person began to manifest and writhe on the floor of the worship centre as the congregation praised the name of Jesus. In this case the worship was continued while the teenage girl was assisted from the premises and given prayer ministry to drive out the spirit.[13]

On another occasion the worship was interrupted just before the sermon. A man in the congregation got up and began to come to the front, informing the congregation as he did so that he was a servant of Satan and wanted to speak. Without batting an eyelid, the worship leader, a very experienced Christian, simply said in a firm voice so that the whole congregation could hear: "In the name of Jesus Christ, I rebuke you, Satan! I command you to leave this place!" Subsequently, the ushers escorted the man from the service. Far from casting a pall over the service, it brought the service to life, because here was an example of a Christian leader who really believed in the power of Christ to challenge and overcome the power of Satan.

---

[11] For example, in recent years the Hillsborough football disaster, the dramatic death of Princess Diana, the 911 terrorist attacks in New York, and the Bali bombings have all stunned and shocked people even though they have known none of the persons involved.

[12] Sometimes in these special situations it may be helpful to work together as a team in leading worship. In other words, other leaders may come forward to lead in prayer, read the Scriptures, give some word of encouragement or guide the direction of the worship.

[13] One must, of course, be careful to differentiate between what is a medical emergency such as an epileptic fit, or mental illness, or spiritual possession. All three are quite distinct and require different assistance. A helpful test for spirit possession is to ask the person to confess: 'Jesus is Lord'.

There is no single blueprint for dealing with all the possible things that can happen, but what is certain is that the leader's response to events is crucial, for it is the leader's response which shows the people in turn how they should respond to the situation. Even within worship leading we need to work out and apply the promise of Scripture:

> '...in all things God works for the good of those who love him....' (Romans 8:28)

Even things that go wrong or are unexpected can be used to bring blessing, if only we do not let the event overwhelm us and blind us to the possibilities.

What Not to Say

It is perhaps also worth considering the things that we ought to avoid saying – specifically the unnecessary, the distracting and the disheartening comments that promote a negative attitude to the worship. If you listen carefully you will be surprised at how often such remarks are made by even experienced worship leaders.[14] Some of these consist of personal remarks that draw attention to the feelings of the leader, some are discouraging or depressing comments that cast a pall on the worship and some are just irrelevant information that distracts from the focus of the worship.

Excuses

Perhaps there is a fine line between an excuse and an explanation but there is a difference. In the context of worship leading, the former is that which seeks to defend the integrity and reputation of the leader, whereas the latter is that which seeks to clarify a situation to remove uncertainty and puzzlement that will otherwise interfere with the worship. All too often leaders and preachers indulge in comments about their personal abilities, the preparation, or their health. Typical of the comments which are heard include:

> "I was only asked to lead the service last night so..."

---

[14] This criticism is also true of preachers who begin sermons with comments about their personal inadequacy to tackle the topic, their failing health which has hindered preparation or the last minute invitation.

Presentation 179

> "The stewards didn't inform me that there would be children present and so..."
>
> "I have rather a sore throat so I hope you will bear with me...."
>
> "This is the final hymn so it doesn't matter if my voice gives out now..."

Almost certainly all of the above comments were true, but what was the purpose? Informing the congregation that you have only been asked at the last minute helps to defend your reputation. If the service is good, then you are an expert at last minute preparation; if the service is a disaster, then you are not the one to blame! Similarly, your justified ignorance of the children's presence absolves from blame for not having prepared a children's talk.

Having a sore throat explains why the congregation will not benefit from the full timbre of your usually excellent resonant voice. Finally, you wouldn't want the congregation to finish the service without knowing what a personal struggle and sacrifice it had been to lead the whole service.

Of course, it is sometimes necessary to provide explanations. The leader or preacher who stands in front of the congregation with a recently broken arm or bandaged head would do well to provide some minimum explanation. This will serve two purposes: firstly, it will prevent the congregation spending the whole service speculating on what happened; secondly, it will save you the trouble of having to give a personal explanation to every worshipper as they leave after the service. But even then, the explanation need not be self-centred. The explanation might be followed by a brief comment of thanks to God for saving from worse injury, or perhaps a spiritual lesson that can be learnt from this vivid visual aid. People will remember because it is an unusual event.

It is only worth drawing the attention of the congregation to vocal difficulties if the information can result in some action. For example, you might use this explanation in order to encourage people to sit closer to the front. To ask the congregation to 'bear with you' sets a negative tone for the worship and leaves people to speculate at what point in the service your voice will finally succumb.

Irrelevance

The comments made by a minister conducting a service of infant baptism are a classic example of this. At every baptism service the minister would publicly produce a thermos flask containing warm water at just the right temperature so as to avoid discomfort to the baby. Having displayed this rather unusual 'Holy vessel', the minister naturally felt duty bound to provide an explanation. Thus, at the point in the service where attention should have been drawn to the significance of infant baptism, the congregation were treated to a little homily on the use of warm water to prevent the baby crying. The idea was ingenious, and the explanation doubtless invaluable to any trainee minister who happened to be present, but distracting for the majority of the congregation.

More typical perhaps is the endless rehearsal of routine notices of events that happen each week. The majority of people do not listen. Those who go to the meetings know what time it is, and those who don't go are much more likely to respond to a personal invitation.

Personal Preferences

Sometimes it can be hard to escape the impression that the service is being conducted as some kind of *Desert Island Discs* show.[15] Thus the service is continually punctuated by comments such as:

> "This is my favourite hymn...."
>
> "I actually prefer (such and such a) tune but...."
>
> "We had this hymn for our wedding..."

Expressing preferences such as these may help to create a 'homely' atmosphere, but at the same time the practice conveys the idea that the service is about the leader and his/her likes and dislikes. Certainly we will have personal favourites but we should not allow them to intrude into our worship leading so as to distract the worshipper from focussing upon God

---

[15] A British radio programme where a celebrity chooses the eight records that he or she would like to be alone with on a desert island. Each choice is accompanied by a reason for the choice.

Disappointments and discouragements

Great care needs to be taken to avoid expressing disappointments from the front or in scolding the congregation for things over which they may have no control. Typical of the remarks which one encounters are:

"I am sorry there are so few here tonight...."

"I had chosen this as a children's hymn but I see there are no children here this morning. We will sing it anyway."

"I am disappointed that so few of you have arrived for the service on time..."

Congregations need to be encouraged not depressed! On one occasion I was leading worship in a small country chapel. In the vestry the steward had already apologised that there were so few members present for the evening worship. However, as I climbed into the pulpit I noticed that there were just 12 members in the congregation. It suddenly struck me that the number was the same as the small group of disciples who had met with Jesus and fellowshipped with Him in the Upper Room. I shared this insight with the congregation at the beginning of the worship and at once our spirits were lifted to worship God. But I could as easily have depressed the congregation by echoing the steward's words of disappointment.

So you had planned a children's talk or a children's hymn and there are no children! Take it in your stride. Either decide that what you had prepared has a message for adults as well and is worth continuing, or change it! Don't draw attention to the lack of children; get on with leading the service.

So you had prepared some beautiful slides to illustrate the prayers of intercessions and the projector bulb has just blown! Hide your annoyance and find some other way to encourage people to pray. Don't entertain the congregation with a sob story that this always happens to you or interpret it as demonic interference. Get on and pray anyway.

Scolding

As a worship leader our role is to encourage and motivate, not to scold and tell off. There is no point in chastising the people who arrive on time with the faults of those who arrive late. If it is a serious problem, bring it up at a later point in the service after the latecomers have arrived and pose your comments as a challenge rather than an accusation.[16]

Similarly, it is quite inappropriate to harangue the congregation at the poverty of their giving or give the impression that the church is on the verge of bankruptcy unless they open their wallets to give generously. Neither will have the desired effect, but both will detract from the idea that the offering is actually a part of worship – something that we tangibly offer to God.

Having the last word

Just occasionally worship leaders cannot resist having the last word – maybe adding some additional comments to the notices or finishing off the sermon.[17] As has already been noted in Chapter Five, particular sensitivity is required in continuing or concluding the worship after preaching so as not to distract from the message. Comments after the message should be very brief and focus on the message and our response, not on the preacher and his ability. It is not a time for a brief summary of the sermon, or some additional points, but an opportunity to respond to God's word.

An appropriate response will of course depend on the tradition of the church and the content of the message, but would normally involve a time of quiet for personal prayer or reflection, a song or hymn of response, or, perhaps, an opportunity for prayer ministry. Ideally the

---

[16] This is a major problem in many churches, especially where the service is very lengthy – two hours or longer. The church leaders need to consider carefully the reasons for late coming. It might be that the service is too long and rather boring, or it could be that it rarely starts on time so people come late to catch the beginning. Very often it is a leadership problem as much as a people problem.

[17] 'Finishing off' can be understood in two senses: firstly, the leader who can't resist adding some additional comments or points or perhaps personal testimony to complete the sermon; or the leader who effectively destroys the sermon by some gross distraction. I have been present on an occasion when the lasting effect of a challenging message was undermined by a worship leader following up the sermon with an amusing anecdote that had absolutely nothing to do with the message.

leader should work with the preacher to bring the worship to a fitting conclusion.

Leading the Singing

Some aspects of this have already been dealt with in earlier chapters, but it is helpful to add one or two comments. To begin with, it needs to be recognised that contemporary worship embraces two quite distinct styles of leading the singing and these need to be discussed separately. Firstly, there is the traditional style where the congregational singing is led by the musician(s) – usually organist or pianist – and the role of the leader is to announce and introduce the hymn. Secondly, there is a completely distinct style where the leader is a proficient singer and it is the leader rather than the musicians who lead and introduce the singing. These two contrasting styles will be discussed briefly below.

Traditional leading style

Normally, providing that the tune is familiar, the leader simply needs to announce or introduce the hymn or song and the organist or musicians then begin to play a suitable introduction, following which the congregation immediately begin to sing.[18] It is not usually necessary for the leader to be a gifted singer, providing that the tunes are well known to the congregation. It is the musicians, sometimes together with a choir, who will lead the congregation.

However, as a leader, unless you have a good singing voice, beware of singing too loudly close to the microphone, since, with modern amplification, you may ruin the congregational singing! In some churches the technician will turn down the volume of the leader's microphone during the singing, but alternatively, the leader can stand back from the microphone, turn it off, or sing quietly although with full expression.[19] If the tune is unfamiliar, or completely new, then some effort needs to be made to teach the congregation. Various options are

---

[18] Normally the organist or pianist will play the melody of the verse, emphasising the final phrase as a preparation for the congregation to sing.

[19] It is important that the leader is seen to sing and hence take part in the worship, but it is not necessary that the leader's voice be heard and, in any event, he should **not** dominate the singing.

possible such as: teaching the song before the service, asking an individual or the choir to sing the song through first, or simply asking the organist to play the tune through a couple of times with the congregation listening carefully and trying to fit the words to the tune.

On occasions, it may be very effective to give some instructions concerning the singing of a hymn. For example, some hymns might be sung in parts or certain verses by men or women only. Alternatively, the leader might request the congregation to sing the song joyfully and enthusiastically, or quietly and prayerfully, perhaps as a song of commitment. Again the hymn might be used as a fellowship song where the people move around the worship centre, greeting one another whilst singing. Or possibly children might lead in actions or provide a danced interpretation of the song.

It is very important that the worship leader should participate in the singing and not have his/her head buried looking for the next item in the service. Advanced preparation will avoid this difficulty. It is also very helpful to look at the congregation while singing and to show relevant expressions on your face. Remember, a gloomy face or dour expression flatly contradicts singing about the 'joy of the Lord'! Be encouraged in your worship by the expressive faces of the worshippers. With experience, you may come to a point where you can also be praying for them whilst singing, longing that they might know the reality of the Lord's presence in their worship.

The Singer-leader

This style of leading has become the norm in many churches where the worship has been influenced by charismatic renewal and the service is led by a worship team. The role of the worship leader here is quite distinct because usually the music group plays an accompaniment rather than the melody line of the song.[20] This means it is the leader who provides the lead-in for the congregational singing and defines the

---

[20] For example, keyboard and guitars usually provide only accompanying chords rather than the tune of the song.

Presentation

tune, rather than the musicians. Thus the worship leader not only leads the congregational singing but also guides the music group.[21]

The advantage of this approach is it enables the worship leader to pick and choose how the song is sung, for example, whether to start with the verse or chorus, or sing the verse several times before introducing the chorus or to sing one line several times *etc*. This makes every singing of the song different and allows the leader more easily to blend one song into another in a seamless series of songs. This can generate a very helpful atmosphere in which the congregation can be caught up in worship and become lost in wonder, love and praise for God.

However, the leader must also plan or think through how songs are going to be used. Sometimes the chorus is not an appropriate introduction to the song as it is based on the meaning of the verse that is planned by the songwriter to precede it. Again, many traditional hymns tell a story, and to pick and mix the verses doesn't make sense of the author's intent. There is also a danger in too much repetition. To sing a line such as 'I love You Lord' over and over again can become a meaningless mantra. Yes, our love for God might be the thought most in our mind or heart, but it may be helpful to find alternative ways of saying it.[22]

When using this leading style the leader must take care not to overwhelm the congregation with the sheer volume of singing. Yes, the leader will lead-in the singing, but after that it should be the congregation's voice that is heard. The leader must also work closely with the music group to ensure that their amplified volume neither drowns the leader nor the congregation. In the seamless type of sequential song presentation, the leader must also work hard to focus

---

[21] The worship leader often has an elaborate system of signs to the music group to indicate repetitions either of a whole verse, the refrain or the last line of the song.

[22] We find many good examples of this in the Bible, especially in the Psalms. For example, Psalm 119, all 176 verses, is about one theme – the Law or the Word of God. The same theme appears in almost every verse, but never in the same way. The psalmist assembles a vast vocabulary to extol God's Law, which in translation is variously referred to as: law, statutes, precepts, decrees, commands, word, and teaching. So too in our praise we need to find alternative ways of expressing the same theme in order to fully understand and plumb its depths.

the people's understanding of the song – somewhat difficult where there is no specific introduction.

The downside of this style of worship leading is that it effectively restricts leaders to those who are musically talented and have a good singing voice. Thus musical ability rather than spirituality or biblical understanding has become, all too often, the essential criteria for selecting a leader. However, one way around this problem is for the worship leader to rely on the back-up singers to lead into the song. The leader can then introduce the songs, provide instructions, read from the Scriptures and pray, whilst relying on others to provide the musical lead. Such lead singers need not, of course, be up 'on stage'; they can be near the front in the congregation where they can be in contact with the leader and musicians.

Summary

The role of the worship leader is a very demanding one, requiring the ability to provide a clear lead but without dominating the worship. The leader's presentation must provide the practical directions for the congregation, generate an understanding of the act of worship, and an encouragement to actively participate. The leader must be able to confidently conduct all the participants in the worship and at the same time cope with the unexpected. The leader must realise that every word spoken is precious and learn how to say things, well and also the kind of things to avoid saying. All of this will come with careful and prayerful preparation as well as on-the-job experience.

11 – Personal

This brief chapter is focussed upon the personal involvement of the worship leader and includes some reflections about beginning to lead worship, and continuing to lead after many years' experience. Whereas, ideally, the leader will be a background figure, enabling the members of the congregation to centre their attentions upon God, nevertheless the leader is not invisible. How the leader feels while leading worship, and his or her attitude to worship, will, however well disguised, be conveyed to the worshippers. Of key importance is whether the leader actually participates in the worship or simply leads others to worship.

Growing as a Worship Leader

The Beginning

Except for professionals such as teachers, lecturers or public speakers who are used to speaking to a group, most first-timers at worship leading find it a daunting experience to stand in front of a congregation. They feel nervous, their legs are like jelly and it seems impossible to unclamp their mouth for the first hesitant syllables. If you feel like this, don't be discouraged; you may still have a gift for worship leading. Three things may help.

First, start simply. Gain experience in leading worship in an informal group such as Sunday School, a youth group or a home fellowship meeting. In the Sunday worship, get used to standing in front of the congregation by reading the Scripture lessons, or leading prayers. Second, be well prepared. Arrive early; make sure you have a complete script for all your worship leading. Share the load with others, *e.g.*, invite other members to read, take prayers *etc.* Third, pray. Thank God for your nervousness, that it is a sign that you are not trusting in your own ability. Seek the Lord's strengthening. Make sure you ask others to support you in prayer and ensure there is someone to pray with you before the service.

Professionalism

After some years' experience of worship leading, whether as an ordained minister, pastor or lay-person, a growing confidence in our own ability may lead to a sense of professionalism. How vital it is that we learn to retain a sense of amateurism[1] – leading because we love to serve God in this way and not because we are paid to do so or feel obliged to do so. We need perhaps to rediscover a sense of 'fear and trembling' as we lead worship. Not now because we are nervous of standing in front of a congregation, but rather we have become aware of the seriousness of our task – to lead worshippers into the presence of a Holy God.[2]

There is perhaps a need to take stock, and maybe reading this book will provide an opportunity to do just that. Are you stuck in a rut? Do you use the same basic material week in week out? Is there variety in the ingredients of your worship? Are you opening up your congregation to new worship experiences? Do you spend enough time preparing? Do you involve others in the worship? Do you work together with the preacher? Are you praying and encouraging others to pray for the worship? Does your worship prepare the way, complement and apply

---

[1] Often people think of amateurish as something second rate or carelessly done – this is not the meaning here. The word amateur is derived from a Latin word meaning to love, and its significance is that an amateur does something because he loves doing it, he enjoys doing it. By contrast, a professional may do her job because it's her obligation or the way to earn a living. Always, as a Christian, our ministry should be done out of love for God and not out of a sense of obligation or duty. (See the biblical view in 1 Cor 13.) Nowhere is this more important than in leading worship.

[2] I started speaking and leading worship in my time as a Science student in Manchester in the Sixties. On the first occasion I spoke, Ian, a senior student, asked me how I felt. I told him I was very nervous. He challenged me over my nervousness and encouraged me to completely trust God. Some months later he again asked me how I felt. The second time, with some experience under my belt, and remembering his earlier comments, I told him I was quite confident. This time he challenged me not to be over confident but to retain a sense of the awesomeness of leading people to worship a Holy God. Ian's challenge and encouragement was timely on both occasions and is something that we could all do well to remember.

the preaching of the Word? Is it living, life-changing, empowering worship?

Humility

One of the key characteristics of an effective worship leader is humility. There is no better example of this than the ministry of Jesus. On the very night that he was betrayed, in the final hours before he was arrested, beaten and condemned to death, he took the role of a servant. [3] The master humbled himself to wash the feet of his disciples, a simple menial task that none of them was prepared to do. This then should be the hallmark of our leading: we seek to serve God through, as it were, washing the feet of the congregation in humblest service.

Our humility will be evident in a number of ways. Firstly, we will seek the help and support of others to pray for our ministry. We will not be ashamed to kneel and be prayed for in times of prayer ministry to seek God's empowerment in our service. Secondly, we will be open to receive comments on our leading and we will sincerely ask others to provide us with an evaluation of how we lead the service. Thirdly, no matter how skilled we become, we will always be modest about our achievements and open to learn more. Throughout our life on earth we remain disciples, that is, those committed to learn from our Lord and Master.

Learning to Worship

One of the hardest things about leading worship is learning to worship. Some leaders are so preoccupied with the task of leading, with what is coming next, that they never actually participate in worship. This is regrettable since it both harms the congregational worship and dries up the spiritual life of the leader. As leaders we need to worship both as an example to others and for own spiritual health.

---

[3] Of course, we should not forget that Jesus' whole ministry was one of service. For example, he taught: "For even the Son of Man did not come to be served, but to serve, and to give his life as a ransom for many." (Mark 10:45) Similarly, Paul attests: "Your attitude should be the same as that of Christ Jesus: Who being in very nature God, did not consider equality with God something to be grasped, but made himself nothing, taking the very nature of a servant..." (Phil 2:5-7)

Three things can greatly help in this area: experience, preparation and participation. Experience in leading provides the confidence so that as a leader you are not overly concerned with what is coming next and so you do not need to keep looking at your notes. Thorough preparation is also key. You should have clearly in your mind and on your service sheet the order of worship and all the necessary materials to hand. The worship leader should not have to spend time searching for a Bible passage or a prayer, whilst leaving the congregation to sing a hymn. These are things that should have been prepared before the service began. Another help is to include others in leading the worship. For each person who reads a Scripture passage, says prayers, or leads a time of praise, there is more opportunity for you to concentrate on the worship. It also involves others and provides them with valuable experience.

Learn to be disciplined in preparing worship. Read and think through hymns/ choruses in advance. In the worship, concentrate on the words and sing them with meaning and conviction. Try to feel and experience the emotions that come through the singing. In times of confession, let the Scriptures convict *you* of *your* sin, know the forgiveness of *your* sin. As you pray intercessory prayers, pray with conviction, long that the Lord will act, that His Kingdom will come. In times of fellowship, be involved. Have eye contact with your fellow worshippers; ask the Lord to pour His love into your heart for them. Listen intently to the Scriptures, the testimony and the sermon; seek to hear the Lord's voice speaking to you. Learn to become, in all respects, a worshipper.

Learning Sensitivity

Learning to be sensitive to the congregation, the worship and the Spirit is perhaps truly a part of the section 'learning to worship', and yet it merits separate attention because it is crucial to *living worship*. Sensitivity is knowing how people feel, reading in their eyes and expressions how the worship is for them. Sensitivity is knowing people, knowing how far change or innovation is helpful and when it will become a stumbling block to worship. Sensitivity is knowing when it is right to invite people to come to the front or to extend a time of silence

Personal

or praise. Sensitivity is an awareness of how the Spirit is working in the midst.

Sensitivity requires flexibility too. Sometimes it may mean a pre-planned flexibility where you have prepared alternative orders of worship depending on the congregation's response. For example, you may have chosen an alternative hymn or song after the message in case the preacher invites the congregation to come forward in response.

Sometimes it is a flexibility thrust upon you, when the Spirit moves so powerfully that the worship takes on a direction of its own and you need to put aside your carefully prepared plans. At times like this you may need help. Other experienced leaders may come forward to interpret what is happening or to pray or to lead in songs of praise and thanksgiving for what God is doing in the midst.

Sensitivity involves knowing how to deal with people; how to pray for the bereaved in such a way as to share their pain and yet reveal to them the joy and certainty of the resurrection. How to cope with an uninvited interruption, or to gently decline an offer of a testimony. How to handle crying babies and distracted mothers. How to speak and lead in such a way as to touch the lives of the worshippers. How to gratefully acknowledge the participation of the helpers and musicians. How to make the stranger and the newcomer feel welcome and at home.

Sensitivity is a complex entity. In part it is derived from our nature, in part it is a gift of the Spirit[4], and in part it is something that can be learnt – very often through the experience of pain and suffering that sensitises us to the pain of others. Discipline yourself to wear other people's shoes. Remember the things you dislike about worship leaders, the things that hurt you and hinder your worship. Determine not to inflict these on others. Get to know the congregation, visit them in their homes, and discover the things that kindle their worship

---

[4] A few have quite remarkable gifts of knowledge (1 Cor 12:8). For example, the evangelist John Sung who ministered in South East Asia had a most unusual gift. The Spirit revealed to him the presence in the congregation of unrepented sin such as adultery, theft or cheating. His gift was much used to bring people to repentance.

experience. Pray that the Spirit of God will make you sensitive to people and the presence of Christ within the worship.

Sensitivity involves being open to opportunities that occur during worship. On one occasion, whilst leading worship, I included a short children's talk and was explaining to the congregation the special role of God's chosen people, the Jews. I was conducting the talk interactively, seeking responses from the children to develop the teaching. At one point I wanted to introduce the concept of the Promised Land and so asked the children to tell me what God had given to His people that was very, very big. I provided various clues but none of the answers got near the point, until finally one five year old child whispered the answer in my ear: "The Holy Spirit!" Now it would have been very easy to ignore her answer, as it was not the one I had been seeking. But it suddenly struck me that she had in fact given a much better answer! What could be 'bigger' or more important than God's Spirit! Instantly mentally binning my 'script', we spent the next few minutes together focussing on this most wonderful of gifts.

Learning to Improve

I hope that your motivation in reading thus far has been to learn something more about worship and leading worship, and that you haven't been disappointed. The willingness to learn betrays an underlying attitude of humility which all of us need to retain throughout our ministry. Sadly, many worship leaders and preachers, having become established or recognised, are reluctant to receive comments from others. This is perhaps especially true in the ordained ministry where comments are perhaps regarded by some as an affront to their professional integrity, or to their call, especially if given by an untrained layperson.

There are, of course, comments and comments! There are the ferociously flung brickbats intended to hurt rather than to help, there are the instinctive reactions, and there are the carefully considered and balanced criticisms given out of a motivation of love. The first are best ignored or maybe followed up in a pastoral context, the second need to be accepted for what they are, and the third need to be actively sought and welcomed. If you are serious about feedback and appraisal then you need to seek it. This means asking one or more persons to listen carefully to your leading and to give some evaluation. If you are under training, then this will probably be done automatically, but if not, then seek a mature Christian who will be honest with you about your leading skills, your strengths and shortcomings.[5]

An additional aid is a video camera. If you can get someone to discretely video your leading during the worship service, then afterwards you can review your leading yourself, taking special note of mannerisms, body language and use of voice.[6] Look out for any unconscious mannerisms that may distract the worshippers.[7] One fairly common problem is lack of eye contact. The leader or preacher looks everywhere: floor, ceiling, walls and doors, but not at the congregation. Some have very poor posture, leaning on the pulpit, slouching, hands in pockets, or unhelpful facial expressions that do little to encourage worship. All these can be detected by video or experienced observations and most mannerisms can be overcome.

Learning to be Inconspicuous

"It's me again!", announced my worship helper to the congregation, as he began to introduce a time of praise. I must admit I writhed inwardly

---

[5] If you are in the position to give evaluation and comments, then try to do so in a positive and encouraging way. Always begin by commenting on the things that were good or well done. There is usually something, even if it is only that the worship leader is smartly dressed or arrived early. If there is really nothing good at all or absolutely no potential, then perhaps suggest that worship leading is not his or her gift. It is often helpful to talk about weaknesses in an indirect way. For example, you can ask their perceptions about their use of voice or the way they announced hymns or prayed. Work together with the leader to identify their weaknesses and always try and suggest ways to overcome them, as well as to further develop their strengths.

[6] Probably the most discrete way is to mount the video camera on a stand and have it focussed on the leading centre. This will pick up most of your leading except when you move out of the sight line. It, however, avoids continuous adjustments that might be disturbing both to you and the congregation.

[7] For example, I never realised until it was pointed out to me that my glasses kept slipping down the bridge of my nose during worship leading and preaching and about every minute I would push them back again. This was completely unconscious on my part but very irritating to some of the congregation. Once you know the problem something can be done about it.

and made a mental note to talk to him after the service. Worship leading is not at all the same as being a compere at a rock concert. In a concert or TV show, extrovert personalities are the norm and the presenter will attempt to attract attention to him or herself by means of garish clothes, meaningless chatter or conspicuous actions. To be a worship leader entails being something of a chameleon – changing one's colours to merge into the background, being inconspicuous so that the congregation can focus on God.

The key to clothes is to dress appropriately. This is clearly quite different for a beach mission than for a formal service. Even in the latter case, what is acceptable varies from church to church and culture to culture.[8] Women leaders in particular need to be careful to dress modestly and appropriately.[9]

Posture and deportment are also important as they help to demonstrate reverence and are a reminder that worship is an important occasion. If we were meeting with the Prime Minister or a king or queen, then almost certainly we would take care how we presented ourselves. Surely this is even more important when we lead others to meet with the King of kings. Even in this increasingly informal age it still doesn't seem appropriate to lead with hands in pockets or slouched against the Communion rail. Similarly, the offering is to the Lord and to casually saunter over to the Communion table or altar, as if to the bank, hardly seems right. At the same time, our movements should never be hurried – we should walk carefully, precisely and reverently.

Words, of course, are equally important. As worship leaders we need to think through carefully the things that we say to ensure that they don't needlessly draw attention to ourselves, as in the example at the

---

[8] The leader should be smart, but what that constitutes will depend on the church, the congregation, and the culture. In Asia, the society including the Christian Church has been greatly influenced by the norms of Western culture. For example, a shirt and tie, or a jacket are increasingly becoming the norm. In my view, this is regrettable because there is always a smart culturally-relevant alternative. Furthermore, to lead or preach in a tie in a tropical climate in a non-air conditioned building is sheer madness!

[9] Consideration needs to be given to how the clothes will perform in action. For example, if the leader is prone to jumping or raising hands during worship, it is worth checking in front of a mirror that her clothing remains modest.

Personal

beginning of this section. In particular we need to be careful about things said on the spur of the moment that we may later regret. Especially avoid making personal remarks about people in public even if you intend it as a joke. It may easily be misunderstood.

When things go wrong

On occasions things may appear to go disastrously wrong. There are a variety of scenarios which most experienced worship leaders will have encountered: the congregation who don't turn up; the absent preacher; the power cut[10]; the non-performing Sunday School; the lack of response at an evangelistic service – the list is endless. There are two things that need be said: firstly, don't take it personally, it is very unlikely that you are to blame[11]; secondly, hold on to the promise of Scripture:

> And we know that in all things God works for the good of those who love him, who have been called according to his purpose. (Rom 8:28)

The above text is essentially Paul's testimony. In one apparent disaster after another he had learnt that God turned the tables and changed failure into blessing. This can happen in our worship when we trust God when things appear to be going wrong.

When things go wrong try to stay calm and think how you can turn the situation around with God's help. It is not actually the end of the world if the preacher doesn't turn up. You can use the sermon time for Bible

---

[10] My worst experience of power cuts was when preaching in wintry Britain. Exceptionally heavy snow, of the *wrong* type, had brought down power lines and the church building had been without power for three days. Not only was the building bitterly cold without any heating, but there were no lights, no organ and not many people! But we still had a good time of worship together even though in a slightly shorter form. I was just thankful that it was a morning service and hence daylight.

[11] The worse possible mistake you can make is to forget that you are leading the service and not prepare or not turn up on the right day. I have done this twice during my 30 plus years as preacher and worship leader and felt really bad about it. The only thing to do is to sincerely apologise, without making endless excuses – there are no excuses! Subsequently try to improve your use of the diary so that it never occurs again. However, although my mistake was inexcusable, it would not have occurred if the local church had contacted me in the week prior to the service. If worship is important to us, then we will make sure to remind the key persons taking part.

study or for testimony or prayer ministry, or reading the Bible.[12] Explain to the people what has happened and what you plan to do. Don't blame the preacher; he may not have forgotten, he may be involved in an accident or seriously ill.

Leading is Time-consuming

Leading worship is a thrilling ministry, but to do it well is very time-consuming. Quite apart from prayer, preparation, planning, and choosing worship ingredients, there is also the contacting and consultation with other participants and the physical preparations such as the worship centre and worship materials. Even with experience, especially if you are involving others in worship or trying something innovative, it will still be time-consuming. But it is worth it! To worship in a church where the worship leader has invested time in preparation, and where the congregation has learnt to take worship seriously, is an uplifting experience. As a preacher, I owe a tremendous debt to those worship leaders who have taken preparation seriously, since a congregation who has really worshipped is a congregation who is receptive to hearing God's word.

Summary

Becoming a worship leader is a daunting experience, but we can all too easily progress from nervousness and a sense of inadequacy to overconfidence and professionalism in our leading. We need to retain a sense of awe at the privilege of leading others to worship, a sense of humility in our ministry, a willingness to listen to others and an openness to learn new things. We need to realise that preparation for *living worship* is time-consuming but it is well worth the effort, as it will bring much blessing to the people.

---

[12] It might be a novel experience and a blessing for the congregation to hear a whole Gospel or some other portion of Scripture publicly read.

Ch 12 - Perspectives

The famous Baptist preacher C.H.Spurgeon was once approached by a lady saying she was looking for the perfect church. Spurgeon's reply was not to invite her to attend his, but to say simply: "Madam, if ever you find it, don't join it, you'll spoil it!" Perfect worship is much like the perfect church in the lady's quest. It does not exist this side of heaven. Our worship is inevitably imperfect and limited because of who we are – sinners saved by grace. This perspective should caution us against thinking that we, or our church, have discovered the ultimate worship experience, or the arrogance to think that we have always possessed it! We need continually to seek how we can grow in our corporate worship and never rest content with where we are now.

Living entities grow, are responsive to stimuli, discard waste and reproduce. They change with time. The same is true of *living worship*. It is a worship which develops and grows; it is a worship that is responsive to people and the promptings of the Holy Spirit; it is a worship that from time to time discards aspects which hinder its life, it is a worship which gives birth to the Kingdom of God in people's lives. Worship must change and adapt, since people, language and cultures change. Although God doesn't change, and the fundamentals of worship remain the same, nevertheless the way we express our worship and the peripheries of worship must change in order for them to be a meaningful experience in the age in which we live.

The original preface of this book drew attention to the worship revolution that has occurred within the contemporary Christian Church worldwide and posed the question whether all is well? In this closing chapter we shall return to this theme and examine some of the strengths and weaknesses of the current worship scene. My hope is that whatever your background or experience, you will read this with an open mind, receiving the comments not as a personal criticism of your own worship style or leadership, but asking yourself what can the Lord teach me that can help my people worship and create truly *living worship* in our midst.

It is clearly not possible to review the whole spectrum of contemporary worship and what is described below must inevitably be something of a caricature. I have chosen to examine contemporary worship under two heads, namely, formal or liturgical worship and free or charismatic worship. Quite clearly these are awkward divisions since there may be charismatic elements within liturgical worship and free worship can sometimes be quite formal, as it may well follow an unwritten order or tradition, but they perhaps help to describe two distinct and influential branches within Protestant churches today.

Formal or Liturgical Worship

This type of worship is found the world over, especially in the mainline denominations such as Anglican, Methodist or Lutheran, where unity within the denomination is strengthened by a common liturgy. Whereas the liturgy may be translated into different languages or revised to make use of more modern idioms, the basic structures tend to be the same. Something of the strengths and weaknesses are discussed below.

Strengths

Biblical foundation

The great strength of liturgical worship is that the liturgy has been carefully prepared with strong biblical foundations. At some earlier time, leaders or founders of the church have set down a general order of service that usually embraces the important aspects of worship and perhaps mirrors to some extent particular emphases within the church. The liturgy reflects the richness of theological insight and at the same time provides the leader with a pattern upon which to model the worship. This safeguards the worshipper from the idiosyncratic and arbitrary formulations of an individual worship leader. Furthermore, a liturgy, used together with a lectionary, ensures that the congregation are exposed to the reading of the Scriptures in a systematic way.

Perspectives

Meaningful

A liturgy is often especially beneficial in the conduct of sacramental services such as baptism or Holy Communion and in occasional services such as marriages or funerals.[1] The liturgy ensures that due emphasis is given to these important worship events and that the meaning of the sacraments, and of marriage and of death are clearly explained. The use of a liturgy also gives a sense of security to the worshippers, who know what is expected of them.

Unifying

Liturgies enable unity at various levels. Firstly, they often provide an historical link with the 'communion of saints'[2] through prayers and creeds that have been created at different periods in history. In humility we recognised the debt that we owe to the great pioneers of faith who brought the Gospel to our own land, and to those who reformed the Church and stamped their mark on the worship. Secondly, the liturgy provides a sense of unity with other Christians worshipping in different local churches within the same denomination and using the same liturgy.[3] Thirdly, liturgies can help create unity and corporate worship within the congregation by providing opportunities for the congregation to join in the worship in saying of responses or reading of prayers. This is a particularly important consideration where congregations are large.

Orderly and balanced

A further positive aspect of liturgical worship is that the ingredients of

---

[1] In the Protestant tradition there are only two sacraments – baptism and Holy Communion, the latter sometimes referred to as the Lord's Supper or the Eucharist. Sacraments are understood as those that are specifically commanded by Christ Himself. (See Mat 28:19 and Luke 22:19).

[2] The 'communion of saints' refers to the fellowship that we have with the whole body of believers both those alive today and those who have preceded us in their pilgrimage of faith. A similar idea to the 'great cloud of witnesses' referred to in Hebrews 12:1. This should be an encouragement and inspiration and a reminder that we are not alone on our earthly pilgrimage.

[3] This is an asset for church members moving to a new town where they can immediately feel at home with the order of service.

worship are ordered in a progressive and logical fashion so that the worship flows from the beginning when we meet with God to a finale when we receive God's blessing and empowerment. It ensures a helpful sequence in worship, for example, confession and forgiveness precede praise, and self-examination precedes receipt of the sacraments. Not only does the worship flow but also it includes all the main elements of worship so as to make a complete and rounded experience.

Weaknesses

Although liturgical worship has many strengths it is not immune from weaknesses such as those described briefly as follows. It will become apparent that many of the weaknesses are not inherent in the liturgy itself but are a consequence of how leaders make use of the liturgy. This is an important point since many of the apparent weaknesses can be overcome by sensitive leadership.

Lifeless

It is vital to realise that liturgy by itself is only a tool which needs to be brought alive to create *living worship*. Many worship leaders are seduced into thinking that a liturgy is a kind of instant service that obviates the need to prepare worship. Nothing could be further from the truth. Certainly a liturgy helps to provide a skeleton on which the worship can be structured, but the leader still needs to wrestle with how to bring the dry liturgical bones to life. The starting point is preparation in prayer as the leader prays through the liturgy. As the service begins, the liturgy comes to life as the leader uses an appropriate tone of voice, pauses in significant places, introduces times of silence for reflection and perhaps explanations or comments that touch on the theme of the service or the meaning of the liturgical text. Life is further infused through the choice of appropriate hymns and choruses, through additional worship events such as giving of testimonies and through opportunities for fellowship such as have already been discussed.

Repetitive

Liturgical worship can so easily become a dead formality, a vain repetition of words and prayers. It is said that 'familiarity breeds contempt' and worship is no exception. Prayers, creeds and responses that are repeated each week can easily become a meaningless ritual. More than that, unless there are any variations or changes, it can become a truly monotonous worship experience. Moreover, unless care is taken to regularly update the liturgy, it may, although theologically sound, become meaningless to the average worshipper. Language is a living entity that changes and so too must our religious language if we are concerned to communicate with people. Furthermore, liturgy assumes literacy and the ability to find your way around service books or service sheets. This can be a daunting experience for newcomers faced with a plethora of service books, songbooks and notice sheets.

Prescriptive

Unfortunately, liturgy often acts as a straightjacket rather than a support since liturgy is seen to prescribe what you *must* do rather than being a springboard for what *could* be done. Thus, attempts to introduce free worship elements into liturgical worship often take the form of an added extra outside of the liturgy, such as a time of praise or singspiration before the worship proper (liturgy) begins. This may act as a form of compromise with traditional elements in the church, but it actually makes nonsense of the liturgy and tends to divide the congregation. If it is deemed desirable to introduce praise choruses, then they should be used within the body of the liturgy where praise is appropriate.[4] If a 'singspiration' is introduced as a preliminary at the start of the service, the usual result is that the more conservative members will begin to arrive late, judging their arrival to coincide with the start of the *real* worship. Thus the *body of Christ* becomes divided.

Expressionless

Perhaps one of the greatest weaknesses of the practice of formal worship is that it is cold. Yes, it is intellectually stimulating, but it provides little opportunity for expression of feeling and for spontaneity in worship. Our praises tend to be channelled through a liturgy that makes little contact with our hearts. We are unable to praise God in our own words or to put our mark on the worship; to own it. We are not

---

[4] If there is no place for praise within the liturgy it needs to be rewritten!

encouraged to use our bodies to express the worship of the Creator. We may sing about the love that we have in Christ, but there is little tangible opportunity for expressing it. Our lives touch one another only tangentially.

Summary

Of course, the above description need not apply to liturgical worship, and there are many churches where it does not, but the dangers are ever present. The constant intent of the worship leader in a formal setting must be to regard the liturgy as a starting point to create *living worship* and not as an instant worship experience to be warmed up and served to the congregation on a plate. This means not only preparation in prayer but also paying attention to the various suggestions described in earlier chapters.

Charismatic or Informal Worship

The modern Pentecostal movement began at the beginning of the Twentieth Century in America and gave birth to churches such as the Assemblies of God. However, in the second half of the century, particularly in the sixties and seventies, the renewal movement escaped the boundaries of specifically Pentecostal churches and began to influence the mainline (liturgical) churches in what came to be known as the Charismatic renewal movement.[5] The distinctive marks of Charismatic worship are the emphasis on praise and the openness to the use of the gifts of the Spirit such as speaking in tongues, prophecy and healing prayer. In more recent times, contemporary concert-style[6] music has also become a key feature in many churches. Some of the strengths and also weaknesses of worship inspired by this renewal movement are discussed briefly below.

---

[5] One of the fascinating features of the Charismatic renewal movement is that its influence has been felt in almost all denominations including the Roman Catholic Church. The movement has had a profound effect on the worship life of the churches involved.

[6] This refers to the use of a concert style format where the leader together with the music group, back up singers and dancers are on stage at the front of the worship centre in a style that is sometimes barely distinguishable from a concert performance.

Strengths

For many the charismatic renewal has provided a completely new worship experience. Some of the positive features are summarised below.

Experiential

If liturgy emphasises a thinking approach to worship, charismatic worship is characterised by heartfelt worship. Within this style of worship the congregation is liberated to express the love they feel for God and encouraged to praise Him. Worshippers are led out from captivity in the arid wastes of intellectualism, from a God who is limited by the capacity of our minds and language, to a God whose overwhelming presence can be experienced. We are given new freedom to praise and there is a sense of excitement in the worship at what God might do in our midst. We use our hands and bodies to express an overwhelming desire to praise and magnify His name. There is opportunity for prayer ministry and healing and an assurance that God can touch our lives. These experiences lead on to a spiral of praise and thanksgiving.

Corporate

The second major strength is that there is a corporate emphasis. The congregation is understood to be the Body of Christ, each member of which has gifts and a role in worship. We are together a Royal Priesthood, called out to declare His praises. So, beyond times of corporate praise in song, there are opportunities for each to share in open prayer, or testimony, or prophecy, thus fulfilling Paul's instruction[7]:

> "When you come together, everyone has a hymn, or a word of instruction, a revelation, a tongue or an interpretation."

At the same time there is usually a very clear acknowledgement that we are together part of the Family of God. There are opportunities to greet one another within the worship and often to minister to one another in prayer. There is a real feel that one belongs, that one really is a brother

---

[7] 1 Corinthians 14:26

or a sister in one large united family. There is an overwhelming sense of God's love being poured into lives and overflowing to others.

Spiritual Gifts

Some would argue that charismatic worship is more spiritual, that within its embrace the congregation is more open to the leading of the Holy Spirit. Certainly there is more freedom to exercise spiritual gifts such as tongue speaking, prophecy, words of knowledge and healing prayer. This does not automatically mean that the worship or the congregation are more spiritual. It is quite clear from Paul's first letter to the Corinthian church that the mere possession and use of spiritual gifts does not make the worship spiritual.[8] Whereas it is perhaps easier to see the Spirit's presence in spiritual gifts, we need also to recognise the Spirit's power at work in a liturgy that challenges the worshipper and in preaching that brings alive God's life-changing word. In the final analysis, what is most important is not so much the style of worship but that we have worshipped, we have communed with God and our lives have been touched and changed.

Weaknesses

Undoubtedly, charismatic worship has revolutionised churches and individual lives and brought great blessing. It has opened our eyes to worship God in a new way. But it is not without its shortcomings, as we shall see below.

Narrow Focus

Perhaps one of the major limitations is the narrow understanding of worship. In brief, worship is equated with praise, and praise in turn is best expressed through song, and the song inevitably must be accompanied by music. This is true to such an extent that singing and music dominate much of contemporary charismatic worship. As a consequence, the ingredients of worship are very restricted to the point that a typical worship order would look something like:

---

[8] Note that Paul was forced to describe the charismatic Christians at Corinth as 'mere infants in Christ' (1 Cor 3:1) and to label loveless ecstatic speech as a 'resounding gong or clanging cymbal' (1 Cor 13:1).

Welcome and Greetings
Opening prayer
Praise
Notices[9]
Preaching
Prayer ministry[10]

Clearly, several aspects of worship discussed in Chapter 3 are missing. There is usually no opportunity for confession[11] as a prelude to praise; there is no assurance of forgiveness and being right with God; often no reading of the Scriptures; no intercession – apart from the prayer ministry; and no final dedication or blessing of the whole congregation before dismissal.

These omissions are serious. There can be no true awareness of the holiness of God, or even the overwhelming presence of the Holy Spirit, that does not make us aware of our sinfulness.[12] Without dealing with that sin, as we do in confession, we are not truly liberated to praise.[13] There must be equal concern that, whereas the Scriptures are honoured in word, they are often neglected in practice. Thus praise takes preference over listening to the Scriptures (there may be no Scripture reading) and prophecy over the preaching from the Scriptures. Similarly, whereas prayer ministry is undoubtedly a breakthrough in experiencing the power of prayer, yet it can be exclusive. Very often, unless the worshipper goes forward to receive prayer ministry, often for

---

[9] These may include the taking up of the offering and welcome.

[10] This may include a further time of praise.

[11] It is interesting that the Charismatic service appears to substitute confession with driving out or binding of evil spirits that might disturb the worship. Both deal with evil but in different ways. Confession implies personal responsibility for the breakdown of our relationship with God; binding evil forces lays the blame on Satan. In the context of worship, whereas there may be demonic forces that intrude, it is probably our personal sin that mostly disrupts our meeting with God and needs to be addressed at the beginning of our worship.

[12] See, for example, Isaiah 6:1-7.

[13] See Psalm 51:14,15 for King David's understanding of the importance of forgiveness as a preparation for praise.

a restricted range of needs, she or he must leave the worship without the benefit of God's blessing on his/her life.

Mindless

In many charismatic churches praise takes the form of an extended period of singing, led by a musically talented worship leader, aided by additional lead singers and accompanied by a music group and frequently a dance team.[14] The period of singing, where hymns are usually notable by their absence[15], may extend for 30-45 minutes or more, whilst the congregation usually remains standing. This time of praise may also include opportunities for clap offerings, shouts of praise, or be interspersed with times of prayer or exhortation by the leader. The effect of this time of praise is uplifting if one allows oneself to become lost in the atmosphere and excitement of the event.

However, such praise does little to stimulate or renew the mind. The praise songs are usually taken from a very restricted corpus and are each repeated, sometimes as many as 5 or 6 times, or more. Furthermore, the words of the choruses tend to be very restricted in scope and are often subjective in nature, expressing how we feel about God, rather than about the nature of God himself. Undoubtedly, such singing, together with impassioned encouragement from the leader to praise God, creates an atmosphere of worship, but is it actually holistic worship?

Free worship exponents object to the vain repetition of liturgical prayers, but fall into the same trap with their repetition of praise choruses. The problem is this: how does a phrase such as: 'I love you Lord' become any more sincere or meaningful the twentieth time it is sung? If they are not meaningful we would do as well to sing: 'La, la, la...'; at least we would not be deceiving ourselves! Perhaps this

---

[14] Positively, there is plenty of visual stimulation, but it is perhaps questionable how far this helps us focus on the presence of God.

[15] Usually songs or choruses are used but on occasions when hymns are used, they are often sung in a way that would not be recognised by their author. For example, the refrain may be sung several times before singing the first or some other verse. The idea that the hymn is telling a story or that the refrain complements the verse is often completely lost.

criticism is best summarised by Paul's comments on the charismatic worship at Corinth:

> "... I will pray with my spirit, but I will also pray with my mind; I will sing with my spirit, but I will also sing with my mind."[16]

How does our singing engage the mind, our powers of thinking and understanding? If it does not, then there is something lacking in our worship. The mind, the spirit, the heart are not mutually exclusive – they need to be integrated so as to bring about holistic worship.

Monotonous

Apart from the potential danger of mindless praise, there are also other technical difficulties with these praise sessions. They can become monotonous because they lack variety in features such as: the type of chorus that is sung, the nature of the musical accompaniment, the level of sound and the need for prolonged standing. Like liturgy, they can become entirely predictable and leader oriented. Perhaps the criticism about the physical endurance that is required in terms of standing and sound level is simply a sign of the author's age, but, be that as it may, there is a need to try and cater for the whole Body of Christ within worship and that must include the not so young.

Sacramental worship

Charismatic worship also seems to have difficulty in coming to terms with the sacramental aspects of worship or with worship tradition. On the one hand, this is seen in the apparent reluctance to make use of corporate prayers such as the Lord's Prayer or the Grace. This is not just a matter of turning our backs upon liturgy, but on prayers used by the saints down through the ages and by the Christian church worldwide. It is turning our back on the Scriptures and even the words of our Lord himself. This is seen too in the celebration of the Lord's Supper, instituted by Christ Himself, and an integral part of the worship of the Early Church, and yet so often marginalized in charismatic worship.[17]

---

[16] 1 Corinthians 14:15

[17] Although, admittedly, even in liturgical worship, the Holy Communion may be tagged on as an extra rather than as a central focus of the worship.

Typically, in a non-liturgical charismatic tradition, a Communion service may consist of 45 minutes or so of praise, 45 minutes of preaching, 30 minutes of prayer ministry and 5-10 minutes for celebrating the Communion. So circumscribed is the time allocated for celebration that there is barely any time other than to distribute the elements and say a prayer of thanksgiving. Frequently, there is no opportunity for self-examination, no attention given to the significance of the celebration, and no opportunity to use the sacrament to cement our relationship as members of the Body of Christ, and to publicly acknowledge the oneness that we have in Him. Without a liturgy we are dependent on the instincts of the worship leader, who, unless he has prepared an order, either makes it up as he goes along, or follows some unwritten tradition. Neither way is satisfactory.

The same kind of difficulties are encountered in the conduct of baptism. It is not unusual at the end of a fulfilling worship service for the pastor to announce that there are to be some adult baptisms. The candidates are then presented to the congregation and are asked to introduce themselves – the pastor doesn't know all their names! There is no time for testimony or for explanation of the significance of baptism. We pray for the candidates and the congregation is invited to attend the actual baptism in the church grounds after the service. Some 15 or 20 minutes later part of the congregation gathers outside to witness the baptisms. The candidates are publicly asked the single, and perhaps ambiguous, catechetical question: "Do you love Jesus?" and then are baptized. As the last candidate is baptized the congregation that had remained disperses.

Again, in this example, the sacrament is marginalized. No explanation is given of its significance and the most important part, the actual baptism, is relegated to after the worship service, whereas, with a little rearrangement of the order of service, it could have been at the heart of the worship. As it was, the worship had already petered out before the baptism and there was no opportunity for the congregation to welcome the newly baptized believers into the *family of God*.

Perspectives

Individualistic

It is perhaps ironic that a movement that gives a renewed emphasis on the corporate dimension of worship can at the same time fall into the trap of individualism. Perhaps this is simply a reflection of modern Western society where the individual and individual rights are of supreme importance. Individualism is particularly marked in song lyrics that generally emphasise the personal (I – God) relationship rather than the corporate (we – God). Thus our praises, our thanksgivings and our prayers become personal rather than corporate expressions of our worship. Individualism is also apparent in styles of prayer – praying with one voice, praying in tongues, and individual prayer ministry. Even the corporate singing can seem individualistic at times when the worship leader's voice dominates the singing or the music group drowns out the congregation.

Certainly we are called to make an individual response of faith to Christ, but on doing so we become members of God's family, His sons and daughters. Our worship needs to reflect this corporate dimension.

Summary

At the heart of this critique is the assertion that worship needs to be mindful. If we dispense with a liturgy, so be it, but we still need to think through our worship. We still need to decide what we are about when we celebrate the Lord's Supper, or baptize new believers, or praise, and we need to be able to explain it to the congregation. Worship still needs to be planned and organized. Without a formal liturgy, the onus is on the leader to plan and direct the worship and not just to muddle through. We have not been given the Spirit so we may abdicate our minds; rather so our minds may be transformed and used more powerfully in His praise.[18]

---

[18] Romans 12:1,2

Conclusion

As I hope is evident from the above comments, in my view, neither liturgical nor free worship hold a monopoly of the truth. In whatever situation we are, we need to strive for balanced, holistic worship. If our worship style is mainly formal and liturgical, we need to be open to the elements of charismatic worship that enable an emphasis on corporate worship, on freeing of the heart, on an exploration of spiritual gifts within worship. If our emphasis is charismatic, we need to rediscover mindful worship and relearn how to take more seriously the scriptural sacramental traditions of the church and, indeed, Scripture itself. Neither is an easy task.

If *living worship* means anything, it means worship that changes. Worship that changes people's lives and is itself neither static nor fossilized. Yes, the God we worship and the principles of worship may not change, but the expression of that worship will, even if it is only because we mature as we grow together into His likeness. One of the hardest things to do as a worship leader is to introduce appropriate change. It is easy to copy others and their worship styles, but worship is not a matter of imitation and externals but of inner reality. May the Lord Himself guide us as we seek to lead our people in worship. May He give us the humility to recognise that we have still much to learn and the ambition to worship together with that great multitude, drawn from every nation, tribe, people and language, before the throne of God in heaven.

Postscript

Biblical worship is essentially about grace – God's unmerited favour freely given to us. From the very beginning God has always taken the initiative. God created, provided, sustained and befriended. God sought wayward women and men to bring them back into relationship with himself. God provided instructions to guide His people and protect society. God sent special messengers (the prophets) to speak on His behalf. Finally, God came Himself in Jesus so that the intimate relationship with his creation might be restored. And as if that were not enough, He sent his Holy Spirit so that those who had never met Jesus might yet know Him, even until this day. In worship we celebrate God's initiative and experience God's continuing grace.

There is perhaps a danger that amidst a practical book on leading worship that we loose sight of the God of grace and initiative. It is perhaps easy to be seduced into thinking that if we put our lives in order, if we prepare well and follow all the tips and suggestions that *living worship* will automatically ensue. If worship were a one-way traffic, involving a single party that would be true. But worship includes a second party – a God of grace and initiative. A God who takes us by surprise like David listening to Nathan's emotive story, like the woman who touched the hem of Jesus' robe, like Peter preaching in Cornelius' home or like Paul and Silas worshipping in the darkness and squalor of a Philippian prison.

Our role as worship leader is to prepare well, but more than that, to be open to God and His surprises. The key to this is prayer. *Living worship* is born in an atmosphere of prayer – leaders who pray, groups who pray, a congregation who prays. We work in partnership with the Holy Spirit in our preparation, our practice and presentation but in prayer we open the door to God's intervention and blessing in our worship and in our lives. Jesus put it vividly in the following words[1]:

> "Here I am! I stand at the door and knock. If anyone hears my voice and opens the door, I will come in and eat with him, and he with me."

---

[1] Rev 3:20

Bibliography

Alexander, Paul (1990) *Creativity in Worship*, Daybreak, DLT, London

Batchelor, Mary (1996) *The Lion Prayer Collection*, Lion, Oxford.

Boschmann, LaMar (1994) *A Heart for Worship*, Hodder & Stoughton, London.

Church of England (1995) *Patterns for Worship*, CHP, London.

Doyle, Dennis (2000) *Creative Arts in Worship*, Hands up for God Ministries, Barrow-upon-Soar.

Draper, Brian and Draper, Kevin (2000) *Refreshing Worship*, Bible Reading Fellowship, Oxford.

Earey, Mark (2000) *Producing your own Orders of Service*, Church House Publishing, London.

Leach, John (1997) *Living Liturgy*, Kingsway, Eastbourne.

Methodist Church (1999) *The Methodist Worship Book*, MPH, Peterborough.

Perham, Michael (1984) *Liturgy Pastoral and Parochial*, SPCK, London.

Richards, Noel (1993) *The Worshipping Church*, Word, Milton Keynes.

Songs of Fellowship: Music Edn (1991) Kingsway Music, Eastbourne.

Walter, Tony (1990) *Funerals and How to Improve Them*, Hodder and Stoughton, Sevenoaks.

Webber, Robert E. (1992) *Worship is a Verb*, 2nd Edition, Hendrickson Publishers, Peabody.

Webster, Rowena (1994) *God's People at Worship – Prayer*, MPH, Peterborough.

White, James F. (2000) *Introduction to Christian Worship*, Third Edition, Abingdon Press, Nashville.